Sexual Minorities in Sports

Sexual
Minorities
in Sports

Prejudice at Play

edited by
Melanie L. Sartore-Baldwin

LYNNE
RIENNER
PUBLISHERS

BOULDER
LONDON

Published in the United States of America in 2013 by
Lynne Rienner Publishers, Inc.
1800 30th Street, Boulder, Colorado 80301
www.rienner.com

and in the United Kingdom by
Lynne Rienner Publishers, Inc.
3 Henrietta Street, Covent Garden, London WC2E 8LU

Library of Congress Cataloging-in-Publication Data
Sexual minorities in sports : prejudice at play /
Melanie L. Sartore-Baldwin, editor.
     p. cm.
  Includes bibliographical references and index.
  ISBN 978-1-58826-890-7 (hc : alk. paper)
  1. Sports—Sociological aspects. 2. Minorities in sports. 3. Sexual minorities.
4. Gays and sports. 5. Masculinity in sports. 6. Feminism and sports.
I. Sartore-Baldwin, Melanie L.
  GV706.5.S49 2012
  306.4'83—dc23

                                                      2012031435

British Cataloguing in Publication Data
A Cataloguing in Publication record for this book
is available from the British Library.

Printed and bound in the United States of America

The paper used in this publication meets the requirements
of the American National Standard for Permanence of
Paper for Printed Library Materials Z39.48-1992.

 5 4 3 2 1

Contents

Sexual Minorities in Sports

1

Gender, Sexuality, and Prejudice in Sport

Melanie L. Sartore-Baldwin

Standing 6-foot 3-inches tall and weighing 226 pounds, professional athlete Gareth Thomas is a rugby legend. He has made the most appearances of any Welsh player, is one of the top scorers in the world, and serves as a leader to his fellow players and a hero to future players and fans. Thomas is particularly well known for his rough style of play that has led to him break many bones (both his own and others'), lose several teeth, and suffer a near-fatal neck injury that resulted in a mini-stroke and almost ended his career. His rough behavior has also been evident off the field. In 2005, Thomas was found guilty of assault after a drunken clash at a French nightclub. Two years later he was banned from rugby for four weeks after forcefully attempting to enter a fan seating area and engaging in hostile exchanges with fans during the 2007 Heineken Cup. Indeed, Thomas's physicality and demeanor communicate that he is big, strong, powerful, intimidating, and by all accounts the epitome of an athlete.

From the outside looking in, Thomas's life appeared to be perfect. He had an incredibly successful rugby career and was idolized by his fans. He was also adored by his wife, Jemma, whom he married in 2001. He was an accomplished athlete, a leader, and a doting husband—the quintessential man. In actuality, however, Thomas had been lying to himself, his teammates, his wife, his family, and the world about who he really was for nearly his entire life. No longer able to hide his secret and suppress his feelings, Thomas announced to the world that he was gay in December 2009. According to *Sports*

Illustrated (Smith 2010), Thomas is the world's only openly gay male professional athlete who is still currently playing a team sport.

Shortly after coming out, Thomas discussed his experiences as a closeted gay man in an interview with the British Broadcasting Corporation (BBC 2009). During this interview, Thomas stated that he had done whatever he needed to do to continue to play rugby and, as a result, had become a "master of disguise." Indeed, Thomas had learned from a very early age that if he wanted to play rugby, he had to be "like the rest of the boys." Thus, beyond possessing exceptional athletic talent, Thomas also needed to act like a rugby player—masculine and heterosexual. To do this, Thomas learned to "act" heterosexual by observing the behaviors of fellow players both on the field and off. For instance, he learned how to act toward women, how to engage in heterosexual locker room banter, and how to ultimately "pass" as a straight man.

Whereas passing as a heterosexual or performing heterosexuality may seem like a harmless way for sexual minorities to avoid persecution, it frequently results in negative physical and psychological consequences (Meyer 2001, 2003). Thomas spoke of feeling immensely guilty for not being honest with loved ones. He also experienced a great deal of confusion, sadness, and isolation as he carried on his charade, as well as suffered physically from the stress of denying his homosexuality to himself and hiding it from others. According to Thomas, the primary reason for enduring this turmoil was so that he could continue to play rugby, and for years the positive experience of playing rugby outweighed all of the negativity associated with remaining closeted. However, amid rumors and after years of hiding, he finally confessed to his wife and a close friend that he was gay. While coming out is different for each and every sexual minority, as are the responses that sexual minorities receive after coming out, Thomas's teammates were supportive of him and his decision to divulge his sexual orientation to the public. Thomas has received some taunting and disparaging remarks, but says that just having people accept him for who he is—a rugby player who happens to be gay, not a gay rugby player—has outweighed any negativity he receives (BBC 2009).

Sports and Society

The story of Gareth Thomas is both unique and common. It is unique in that Thomas is an openly gay professional rugby player who has continued to play his sport since coming out. Other professional athletes have also come out, but have done so toward the end of their careers or after retiring (e.g., Justin Fashanu, John Amechi, Esera Tuaola). Thomas's story is common in that it refers to several historically based cultural and contextual constraints within the context of sport. From its inception, sport has been a site where traditional gendered roles are embraced (Messner 1992, 2002). Relatedly, sport has long been a context in which members of certain social groups or categories possess more power and status than others (e.g., Knoppers et al. 1990, 1991; Messner and Sabo 1990). As a result, the wants and needs of members within these groups have been and continue to be the most valued and privileged. What is perhaps most fascinating about this phenomenon is that even though society's definition of sport has evolved and changed over time (Coakley 2009), the groups driving these changes have changed very little. A brief discussion of the history of sport highlights this claim. While a complete history is beyond the scope of this chapter and book, a great deal of insight can be gained from a few examples. Indeed, "the person who studies sport without studying its history will never truly understand any given state of sport or the forces operating to change it" (Sage 1998:7).

It is common knowledge that the first Olympic Games were dedicated to the Greek god Zeus. The celebration incorporated games and events that resembled the socially acceptable behaviors and activities of young, able-bodied males who were often wealthy and affluent (Coakley 2009). Women, older men, persons with disabilities, and all others who had lower social standing were viewed as inferior and were not allowed to compete. In fact, women were not even allowed to attend or view the games, which thus reasserted and maintained their subordinate status. While the Olympic Games have evolved into something much more inclusive, a great number of the original traditions were carried over to the first "modern" Olympic Games, in 1896. Women, for example, were not allowed to officially compete until 1932. To this day, athletes with physical disabilities are still differentiated, as they compete in a separate Olympic event, the Paralympics.

As another example, within ancient Roman society, sport took the form of dangerous fights between Roman gladiators and wild animals. Watching and placing wagers on gladiator events also became a form of sport, as it was a source of mass entertainment. The gladiators were not generally willing competitors, however. They were often criminals or property of the wealthy and were forced to fight animals and other Roman gladiators to the death. Even female slaves were forced to compete against wild animals. Women of affluence, however, were not forced to compete but were allowed to attend and cheer. Perhaps most important, all of the decisions about what events comprised the Roman spectacles and who competed in and attended them were made by government leaders as a way to control other segments of Roman society. Indeed, the Olympic Games were constructed and used in much the same way.

Many of the ideas that surrounded ancient sport still surround modern sport, which to a large extent remains stratified by and structured around ideological belief systems. The story of Gareth Thomas illuminates how the ideologies surrounding sport, gender, and sexual orientation can result in stigmatization, prejudice, and discrimination (e.g., Anderson 2005a, 2009; Sartore and Cunningham 2009a, 2009b; Cunningham, Sartore, and McCullough 2010). The purpose of this book is to explore these constructs within the context of sport from a variety of vantage points. First, however, an introduction to the concepts of sexual stigma and sexual prejudice is necessary.

Sport and Sexual Prejudice

Sport has long been utilized to socialize and reinforce traditional gender roles for men and women of all ages (Griffin 1998; Harry 1995; Pronger 1990). Because of this, challenges to patriarchal ideals through the crossing of gender boundaries have historically elicited negative attitudes toward the presence of nonheterosexuals in sport (Anderson 2002, 2005a; Griffin 1998; Krane 1997). The presence of females, femininity, and nonhegemonic forms of masculinity within sport highlights the perceived mismatch between the sociocultural gender stereotypes found within the sport context. Almost certainly, female and male athletes who do not conform to the idealized standards of femininity and masculinity are not only devalued but also stigmatized (Connell 1987, 1995; Griffin 1998; Kolnes 1995; Krane and Barber 2003; Shaw and Hoeber 2003).

Whereas the term "homophobia" has long been employed to describe negative attitudes toward homosexuals, contemporary theorists and researchers have begun to stray away from its usage. Homophobia was first defined by psychologist George Weinberg as "the dread of being in close quarters with homosexuals—and in the case of homosexuals, self-loathing" (1972:4). This clinical definition is limited in that it centers on an "intense fear" of homosexuals, focuses only on the individual level, overlooks societal-level prejudices, and focuses primarily on homosexuality, specifically gay men, rather than sexual orientation as a larger spectrum (Herek 2000, 2004). In light of these shortcomings, Gregory Herek advanced the term "sexual prejudice," which comprises "all negative attitudes based on sexual orientation" (2000:19), as a more appropriate way to refer to negative attitudes toward sexual minorities.

Sexual prejudice is manifested from one's internalization of society's negative regard for sexual minorities, or sexual stigma (Herek 2009). A stigma reflects culturally shared knowledge about members of a specific social group and comprises labeling, stereotyping, separation, status loss, and discrimination (Link and Phelan 2001). Stigma establishes power differences between groups that maintain and even enhance the in-group/out-group distinction and maintain social hierarchies (Sidanius et al. 2001; Tajfel and Turner 1979). Stigma legitimates the power and status differentials that exist within society (Link and Phelan 2001). Because sexual stigma encompasses both gender and sexual orientation, it is evident across all social institutions and therefore reinforces the profound presence of sexual prejudice.

Sexual prejudice is a negative *attitude* held toward individuals, groups, and communities based on perceptions of nonheterosexuality (Herek 2000). It is not an emotion or a behavior but rather a response to cognitive information about sexual minorities. This information usually takes the form of stereotypes that have been formed in relation to gendered heterosexual norms (Herek 2009). Heterosexuality has long been constructed as the norm and subsequently embedded as such across numerous social institutions (religion, law, sport, etc.). Referred to as heterosexism, or the social ideology that characterizes nonheterosexual behaviors, identities, relationships, and communities as deviant and abnormal, this structured form of sexual stigma reaffirms the devaluation of nonheterosexuals by promoting the assumption of heterosexuality (Herek 2009). Heterosexism also maintains the stigmatization of sexual minorities by upholding the differences in status and power possessed by nonheterosexuals relative to their heterosexual counterparts (Herek 2009; Link and Phelan 2001).

Several researchers have identified the realm of sport as a heterosexist institution organized by heteronormativity and hegemonic masculinity (Anderson 2002; Connell 1995; Hargreaves 2000; Sartore and Cunningham 2009a, 2009b). Given this, sexual stigma is therefore present in sport. Sexual prejudice has also been identified and has been found to influence the behaviors of both heterosexuals and nonheterosexuals in the context of sport. George Cunningham and I (Sartore and Cunningham 2009a), for instance, have found that sexual prejudice influences the decisions of athletes and their parents regarding participation in sports. Athletes rely heavily on stereotypical beliefs, formed on the basis of heterosexist gender norms, when explaining their participation decisions. Specifically, they rely on negative stereotypes of gays and lesbians.

Stereotypes

A stereotype is a "set of beliefs about the personal attributes of a group of people" (Ashmore and Del Boca 1979:16) and can serve to communicate a level of devaluation associated with specific social identities (Crocker, Major, and Steele 1998; Davies, Spencer, and Steele 2005). Negative stereotypes can therefore be determinants of negative attitudes (i.e., prejudice) toward specific groups (Allport 1954; Dovidio et al. 1996; Fiske 1998). Additionally, the very nature of stereotypes suggests that simply being aware of them serves to bias the interactions with and behaviors toward members of stereotyped and stigmatized groups (Devine 1989). This is not to blame individuals for stereotyping, however, as the process itself is highly efficient and functional. When one is presented with a target person or persons, cognitive resources are conserved through the activation of automatic, contextually relevant categorizations and stereotypes (Devine 1989; Fiske 1998; Rush 1998). Recall of additional information, once activated, is likely to be congruent with stereotypes.

Prevailing cultural stereotypes are evident at very young ages and have been found to influence personal interactions and general attitudes throughout one's life (Aronson 2004; Rowley et al. 2007). Thus they influence the prejudices people possess. For example, stereotypes of gays and lesbians have been found to be highly influential in the formation of homophobia and sexual prejudice (Bernstein 2004; Herek 2000, 2009). The often undifferentiated relationship between homosexuality and pedophilia (Plummer 2006), and stereotypes of gay males that revolve around beliefs of sexual obsession, promiscuity, femininity, flamboyance, and perversion (Bernstein 2004; Simon 1998), are quite damaging. Equally unfavorable, stereotypes of lesbians embody beliefs of sexual seduction, unwanted predatory advances, masculinity, aggressiveness, and harmfulness toward children (Eliason, Donelan, and Randall 1992). Indeed, both sets of stereotypes provoke sexual prejudice in some and reinforce it in others (Herek 2009).

Historically, male heterosexuality has been assumed and rarely questioned in sport, while the opposite has been true for females (see Griffin 1998). The preservation of male dominance and power in sport through the imposition of gender-appropriate behaviors for both men and women has, to a large part, maintained this dynamic (Kolnes 1995; Krane 2001; Messner 1992). From the masculine ideal of the athlete (i.e., pure power, strength, and assumed heterosexuality; see Messner 1992) to the prototypical identity of the sports coach (i.e., white, Protestant, able-bodied, heterosexual male; see Fink, Pastore, and Riemer 2001), those who participate within the realm of sport bear no resemblance to the gender-based, stereotypical notions of homosexuality. While recent research has suggested cultural shifts (e.g., Adams 2011; Kian and Anderson 2009), there remains incongruence between the meanings and beliefs surrounding nonheterosexuals and the heterosexist cultural norms within sport.

Stigma

The heterosexist structure of sport and sport organizations suggests that sexual stigma is not only present but also somewhat sanctioned. Several investigations within the sport context support this supposition and suggest that men and women, heterosexual and nonheterosexual, all possess some level of awareness and expectation in relation to sexual stigma (Anderson 2002, 2005a; Sartore and Cunningham 2009b, 2010). Research has demonstrated that this expectation of negativity or prejudice, referred to as "felt stigma" (Goffman 1963; Herek 2009), can be detrimental to one's overall health and well-being (Smith and Ingram 2004) as well as influential within one's work and personal life (Brooks 1981; Crocker and Major 1989). Research also suggests that when persons hold expectations of prejudice and discrimination, they may adopt identity management strategies and coping mechanisms in an effort to avoid the effects of being stigmatized (Beatty and Kirby 2006; Crocker, Major, and Steele 1998; Major et al. 1998; Pinel 1999; Pinel and Paulin 2005).

While the invisible nature of one's sexual orientation may allow sexual minorities to escape physical violence and verbal assaults, the stress of being stigmatized and the fear of confirming negative stereotypes can be both psychologically and physically harmful (Brooks 1981; DiPlacido 1998; Dworkin and Yi 2003; Meyer 2003; Lewis et al. 2006). Research has consistently demonstrated that identifying as a sexual minority can lead to stress, referred to as "minority stress," that is harmful to health (Meyer 2003). Ilan Meyer (1995), for instance, reported that the gay males in his study, as targets of societal discrimination, experienced negative mental health outcomes. A more recent meta-analysis revealed that sexual minorities were 2.3 times more likely to suffer from a mental disorder than their heterosexual counterparts (Meyer 2003). Behaviorally, minority stress may also result in substance abuse, suicidal tendencies, and depression for sexual minorities (DiPlacido 1998; Fingerhut, Peplau, and Gable 2010; Meyer 1995, 2003). Minority stress can also threaten one's performance as a result of the fear of confirming negative stereotypes about one's social group (Aronson 2004).

As Herek (2009) noted, "stigma consciousness" is one manifestation of felt stigma. Stigma consciousness is the response to a devalued identity and its domain-relevant stereotypes being made salient (Pinel 1999). More specifically, it is the degree to which persons focus on their own stereotyped status within given contexts. Within the United States, numerous societal stereotypes exist. For instance, African Americans are likely aware of negative stereotypes regarding their purported intellectual inferiority and aggressive dispositions (Crocker, Major, and Steele 1998). Likewise, the prevailing stereotypes revolving around women's purported excessive emotionality, poor math skills, and leadership abilities are not likely to escape the consciousness of females (Crocker, Major, and Steele 1998; Davies, Spencer, and Steele 2005). Sport-related gender stereotypes also exist and have been found to be salient and influential in the participation decisions made by young boys and girls (Schmalz and Kerstetter 2006, 2008). Specifically, it has been shown that young boys are acutely aware of the necessity to exude masculinity while engaging in sport and, as such, feel confined to behave in a masculine manner. Girls, on the other hand, perceive more freedom in their behaviors and thus behave in both feminine and masculine ways. These findings are consistent with other research identifying sport as a heterosexist institution in which stigma and stereotypes inform behaviors and actions (Griffin 1998; Harry 1995; Messner 1988; Zipp 2011).

Another manifestation of felt stigma is "stereotype threat," or the risk of confirming the negative stereotypes about one's social group through one's own behavior (Spencer, Steele, and Quinn 1999; Steele and Aronson 1995; Steele, Spencer, and Aronson 2002). Accordingly, the higher one's awareness of stigma and associated stereotypes, the more likely that stereotype threat is to occur. Stereotype threat can result in both acute and chronic behavior modifications with the intent of disconfirming stereotypes and avoiding stigmatization (Conley et al. 2002; Crocker and Major 1989; Major and O'Brien 2005; Steele, Spencer, and Aronson 2002). It can also be characterized as a hypervigilant state whereby dedicating mental and physical attention to the disconfirmation of salient stereotypes can result in diminished performance. In their study of gay men, for example, Jennifer Bosson, Ethan Haymovitz, and Elizabeth Pinel (2004) demonstrated a performance detriment when sexual orientation was made salient. Specifically, in their experiment comparing the childcare skills of gay and heterosexual men, gay men whose sexual orientation was made salient performed poorer than gay men whose sexual orientation was not made salient. Bosson and colleagues concluded that performance differences were the result of stereotype threat. Specifically, the gay men whose sexual orientation was made salient were trying to avoid the stereotype of gay male as sexual predator (Freedman 1995; Plummer 2006). While unfounded, this stereotype has also informed attitudes toward gay men as teachers of young children (King 2004). The same stereotype could also be evoked when a male sport coach is identified as gay (Sartore and Cunningham 2009a). Because of this, sexual minorities within the sport context often choose to manage the extent to which they disclose their sexual orientation (e.g., Sartore and Cunningham 2010). The story of Gareth Thomas provides an example of such identity management.

Outline of the Book

The subsequent chapters in this book explore and explain the complex relationships between gender, sexual orientation, and sport from different vantage points. In Chapter 2, E. Nicole Melton adopts a multilevel perspective and draws upon several areas of literature to discuss the ever-present lesbian stigma found in sport. In Chapter 3, Eric Anderson, Mark McCormack, and Matt Ripley discuss gay males in sport. Specifically, these authors explore the evolution of homophobic language in the sport context, as it relates to changing attitudes. They identify homophobic language as a reason for challenging the notion that the realm of sport is the last bastion of homophobia and sexual prejudice. In Chapter 4, Erin E. Buzuvis discusses the transsexual and intersex athletes. With an emphasis on policy, she highlights the manner in which the individual's right to self-define his or her gender identity has long served as a stigmatizing force in sport. In Chapter 5, Nefertiti Walker explores the multiple minority status of African American sexual minorities. Recognizing that gay, lesbian, bisexual, and transsexual African Americans possess both visible and invisible characteristics that are devalued in the heterosexist environment of sport, she addresses the need for a better understanding of the effects of confounded prejudices.

The next two chapters discuss both practical and theoretical ways in which prejudices have been broken down and how sexual minorities have been empowered in the sport context. In Chapter 6, Caroline Symons provides a detailed historical account of the Gay Games and discusses how they have become a site where both diversity and unity are valued. She provides several accounts from Gay Games participants and organizers that highlight the effect of the games on the gay, lesbian, bisexual, and transsexual community. In Chapter 7, George B. Cunningham discusses the benefits of sexual orientation diversity within sport organizations. Drawing upon the social categorization framework (Tajfel and Turner 1979; Turner et al. 1987) and various literatures, he presents an integrated framework that highlights the processes necessary for sport organizations to benefit from and provide a benefit to sexual minority employees. Finally, in Chapter 8, I conclude the book offering suggestions for the future of sexual minorities in sports.

2

Women and the Lesbian Stigma

E. Nicole Melton

In 2007, Sherri Murrell was named the head women's basketball coach at Portland State University and immediately started to make an impact on the program. Under her leadership, the Vikings posted their four most successful seasons as a National Collegiate Athletic Association (NCAA) Division I member, which included a berth to the 2010 NCAA Championship Tournament. During the 2010–2011 season, Coach Murrell led her team to its first regular-season conference title and deservedly received the Big Sky Conference Coach of the Year award. While the success of the women's basketball team has certainly been the subject of many newspaper headlines, Coach Murrell's personal life has perhaps received the most attention in terms of national media coverage (Bachman 2011).

This interest stems from a decision Murrell made prior to the 2009 season. Specifically, the assistant media relations director asked Murrell if she wanted to include a family photo in the team's media guide. Without hesitation, Murrell agreed and a picture of the coach and her partner, Rena Shuman, each holding one of their fraternal twins, was uploaded to the university's athletics website. Though references to a coach's family are commonplace in women's basketball, and sport in general, this image sparked national attention because Murrell became known as the only publicly lesbian coach in Division I women's basketball—a title she still holds today.

Of course, Sherri Murrell is not the only lesbian coach in Division I women's basketball. This is evidenced by the numerous letters, phone calls, and e-mails she receives from closeted lesbian coaches who express their desire to publicly disclose their sexual orientation. However, the realm of sport is typically not a setting where women feel they can challenge traditional notions of gender, femininity, and sexuality. Rather, regardless of their sexual orientation, women often believe they must present themselves in stereotypical feminine ways, advertise their heterosexuality, and adhere to traditional gender norms in order to gain acceptance and achieve success in sport—a context characterized by patriarchal traditions of heteronormative masculinity and male hegemony. Thus these women abide in a culture of silence, fearful of the consequences associated with being labeled a lesbian (e.g., public stigmatization, becoming the target of negative recruiting tactics, or job termination; see Krane 1997; Sartore and Cunningham 2009b).

Given the numerous advances in terms of gender equality in sport, it may seem surprising that many women feel they must act in accordance with traditional gender norms and conform to this code of silence. However, by many accounts, the mere presence of women in sport is seen to violate patriarchal ideals and consequently makes women the target of discrimination and stigmatization. Thus the purpose of this chapter is to discuss how prevailing views regarding gender, femininity, and sexuality maintain and perpetuate the devalued position women hold in sport. Specifically, I draw from Melanie Sartore and George Cunningham's (2009b) conceptualization of the lesbian stigma to illustrate how sexual prejudice acts as a powerful force in limiting the opportunities, experiences, and status of women in sport. I begin by defining relevant concepts and examining the various societal, organizational, and individual factors that leave women vulnerable to the lesbian stigma. Next, I identify various consequences and outcomes associated with this form of stigmatization. Finally, I discuss possible moderators that may intensify or diminish the negative effects related to the lesbian stigma. Figure 2.1 offers an illustrative summary of the concepts and relationships outlined in the chapter.

The Lesbian Stigma in Sport

It is important to understand the difference between the term *sex* and the term *gender.* With respect to the first, sex and sex differences relate to biological characteristics, such as one's chromosomal compo-

Figure 2.1 Antecedents of the Lesbian Stigma in Sport

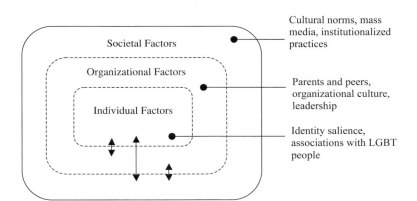

sition or genitalia that are ascribed to females and males. Though people sometimes use the terms *sex* and *gender* interchangeably, gender and gender differences refer to the set of gender norms or practices that are considered to distinguish between women and men, correspond with one's biological sex, or reflect one's gender identity. As Judith Butler (1990) describes, the concept of gender has come to contain the specific gender roles that are deemed appropriate for women and men. Within Western societies, women are expected to be an example of femininity, whereas men must embody the traits and characteristics associated with masculinity in order to achieve power and prestige in society.

Historically, gender has also been linked to one's sexuality, which for the purposes of this chapter can best be conceptualized as a mixture of sexual behaviors, attractions, and fantasies (Gosiorek and Weinrich 1991). People may share these feelings and behaviors with members of the opposite sex, the same sex, or both sexes. However, traditional gender beliefs contend that in order to be feminine, a woman must be attracted to men, and in order to be masculine, a man must be attracted to women (Krane 2001). Holding this dichotomous view of gender and sexuality has considerable implications for those who work or participate in the sport context.

In sport, traditional views of gender, gender roles, and sexuality are used as organizing principles to reinforce male superiority, female subordination, and norms of heterosexuality (Krane 2001). As such, research continually characterizes the realm of sport as a site that produces and perpetuates masculine and heterosexual dominance (Messner 2002). Within this gendered setting, white, Protestant, able-bodied, heterosexual males are considered to embody the characteristics of the prototypical sport employee or participant, and are subsequently afforded greater power, privilege, and status than those who do not resemble this prototype (Fink, Pastore, and Riemer 2001). Men will exhibit hyper-masculine traits in order to improve their status in sport; however, women, seen as trespassers in this masculine domain, must perform hyper-feminine behaviors as a way to gain limited acceptance from members of the dominant group (i.e., prototypical sport employees and participants). Furthermore, the norms of masculinity and femininity are coupled with the assumption of compulsory heterosexuality (i.e., all individuals are or should be heterosexual; Rich 1980). Those who deviate from any of these expected forms of behavior are likely to face discrimination and stigmatization—with women in sport being particularly vulnerable to this type of negative treatment (Sartore and Cunningham 2009b).

When examining the reasons why a woman experiences discriminatory treatment, one must be mindful of the fact that heterosexuality is an organizing principle in women's sport. That is, perceptions of heterosexuality determine how a woman is viewed in sport, which means that whether a woman is accepted or rejected is particularly dependent on whether she is considered feminine or masculine, heterosexual or homosexual. Thus, according to Sartore and Cunningham, "the lesbian label exists within sport's heterosexist and heteronormative context as a means to subvert women's status, power, influence, and experiences" (2009b:289). Those who have been ascribed with this stigma generally face significantly lower status, discrimination, and prejudice. In order to understand specific components of the lesbian stigma, it is necessary to outline the antecedents and outcomes of the stigma, as well as discuss possible moderators to these relationships.

Antecedents of the Lesbian Stigma

Sport organizations are complex, multilevel systems (Chelladurai 2009), and it is oftentimes advantageous to adopt a multilevel perspective when examining social phenomena in sport. In line with systems theory (Chelladurai 2009; Kozlowski and Klein 2000), this approach argues that social phenomena are best understood when one considers factors at the macro (societal or cultural), meso (organization or team), and micro (individual) levels. Furthermore, the factors at each level can influence one another, such that certain micro-level factors may form because of macro- or meso-level contexts, and individual attitudes and behaviors may collectively shape societal norms. By acknowledging these complexities, multilevel theorizing allows for a more complete, holistic understanding of organizational processes.

The benefits of multilevel theorizing are also evident when seeking to understand antecedents of the lesbian stigma. Factors at the societal (macro), organizational (meso), and individual (micro) levels all influence if and when the lesbian label is used to marginalize women in sport.

Societal Factors

Societal or macro-level factors that influence sexual stigma are elements that are external to a specific sport organization or team, but that may still exert considerable influence on individuals within these contexts. These macro-level factors include cultural norms, mass media, and institutional practices.

Cultural norms. Individuals rely on cultural norms to help them make sense of the world and successfully navigate through various social settings. Norms allow people to identify what behaviors, preferences, and attitudes are deemed acceptable in a given context (Coakley 2009). As such, prevailing norms in society can shape how people view women and sexual minorities in sport. For example, traditional gender beliefs still influence the attitudes and actions of people in modern societies. As discussed previously, femininity and masculinity are associated with socially constructed standards for women's and men's appearance, behavior, and values (Bordo 1993). And while multiple forms of femininity and masculinity may exist, generally one privileged or hegemonic form will emerge and will subsequently be afforded more power and greater status. For instance, women who appear slender, toned, and graceful, or who display passive or nurturing personality traits, generally embody the hegemonic form of femininity, whereas the hegemonic, masculine male would be self-confident, aggressive, strong, tall, and muscular. These views carry over into the sport context and dictate what roles are appropriate for females and males through gendered language, policies, and practices (Krane 2001). As such, it is only acceptable for women to play sports that highlight their beauty and grace (e.g., gymnastics, figure skating) or sports that require limited physical contact (e.g., tennis, golf, volleyball).

As another example of cultural norms, consider that the stigma associated with being, or perceived as being, lesbian, gay, bisexual, or transgender (LGBT) is still pervasive and powerful in society, and negatively affects those subjected to it. Indeed, national surveys show that a significant portion of adults consider homosexuality as "always wrong" (see Herek 2009), and adults' attitudes toward sexual minorities are routinely less positive than they are toward other minority groups (Gill et al. 2006; Herek 2009). Furthermore, whereas other forms of prejudices face public criticism and condemnation, such as sexism or racism, it is often socially acceptable to overtly express sexual prejudice (Herek 2007, 2009). Consequently, sexual minorities continue to face discrimination and prejudice across a number of contexts.

These attitudes can also influence how sexual minorities are perceived in sport settings. Indeed, research suggests that people who participate in sport and exercise generally hold negative attitudes toward sexual minorities. Furthermore, Sartore and Cunningham (2009a) observed that parents are reluctant to allow their children to play for teams led by lesbian and gay individuals, and athletes do not wish to play for lesbian and gay coaches. Research suggests that sexual prejudice among decisionmakers in sport also negatively affects hiring recommendations for sexual minorities (Cunningham, Sartore, and McCullough 2010). Collectively, these studies suggest that the cultural norms within a certain context can shape the prevalence of heterosexism and the specific sexual prejudice that individuals encounter.

Mass media. Various forms of media, such as television, social networks, radio, print, and the Internet, significantly influence individuals and society as a whole. In fact, research suggests that the media constitute "one of the most powerful institutional forces for shaping values and attitudes in modern culture" (Kane 1988:89). The images and themes promoted in the media can—implicitly and explicitly—influence one's feelings toward various subjects, change how one thinks, and even shape one's views concerning the roles men and women should hold in society (Melton 2010b). This is certainly the case in sport, as research examining the coverage of male and female athletes suggests.

In terms of media coverage, a number of scholarly investigations examine the differential treatment of women's sport when compared to men's (see Melton 2010b). For instance, male athletes and men's athletic competitions are given disproportionately more attention than female athletes and women's athletic competitions. The media portray men's sport as exciting, fast-paced events played with superior athleticism—themes that rarely appear in coverage of women's sport. Rather, when women are covered in the media in relation to sport, they are often depicted in sexualized ways or shown in supportive roles, such as the girlfriend or wife of a male athlete. These representations reinforce the notion that sport constitutes a male domain and women are only permitted to enter if they conform to traditional gender roles.

Though it may not be obvious, these images reinforce the lesbian stigma by maintaining the norm of heterosexuality in sport (i.e., all females are feminine and heterosexual). As one illustrative example, consider the commentary during the 2011 Women's World Cup in Germany. Every time US defender Christie Rampone touched the ball, the announcers reminded the audience that she was formerly Christie Pearce and was now the mother of two children. Perhaps they felt the need to repeat this fact over and over again because Rampone was actually the only mother on the 2011 team (Wahl 2011). Though no derogatory remarks were made in regard to lesbianism, it was evident that being married to a man and having children was the valued norm—there was no mention of Abby Wombach's (a notable lesbian player on the team) partner or family.

Institutionalized practices. Activities and practices within an organization are said to be institutionalized when, as a result of habits, customs, and traditions, they become standardized or take on a rulelike status (Meyer and Rowan 1977). These processes become so ingrained in "the way things are done" (Scott 2005) that those in the organization unquestionably accept them, and actually start to reinforce these institutional norms because they are seen as legitimate and necessary (Washington and Patterson 2011). In the sport context, gender discrimination is said to be institutionalized because of the history, tradition, prevailing stereotypes, and lack of legal enforcements.

In regard to the current discussion, institutional norms related to gender and sport can also result in enactment of the lesbian stigma in sport settings. For instance, consider the culture of silence discussed in the story of Sherri Murrell that opens this chapter. Though it is not uncommon for gay and lesbian individuals to conceal their sexual orientation at work, the code of silence in women's sport is particularly prevalent. It has become an unquestioned standard in sport that women, regardless of sexual orientation, must prove their heterosexuality, and lesbians are required to stay in the closet for the "good of the game" (Plymire and Forman 2000:142). The code of silence emanates from the taken-for-granted assumption that "out" lesbians are dangerous and something to be feared—fans and sponsors would shun these women and abandon women's sport entirely if homosexuality were allowed. Consequently, many female athletes, coaches, and administrators who have revealed their sexual orientation, have been outed, or have merely been suspected of being lesbian have lost their jobs (Griffin 1998). Unfortunately, it does not appear that women are making any strides toward ending this oppressive culture. As Pat Griffin (2007) stated:

> I've been noticing lately how many heterosexual men in sport—coaches, athletes, pro team GMs [general managers] have been speaking out to support LGBT athletes, school anti-gay bullying programs and broader LGBT issues like marriage rights. NFL players, Brendan Ayanbadejo, Scott Fujita, Antonio Cromartie, Drew Brees; NBA players, Manu Ginobli and Steve Nash; MLS player, Mike Chabala; Ohio State Football coach, Jim Tressell, NCAA Wrestling Champ, Hudson Taylor; Toronto Maple Leafs GM, Brian Burke; former NFL commissioner, Paul Tagliabue; and others I have missed have all spoken out publicly. When I try to name one heterosexual coach of a woman's team or college or professional athlete who has spoken out in similar ways, I am stumped. The silence is deafening.

The absence of women in the campaign for LGBT equality is striking. In many respects it highlights the immense fear associated with being labeled a lesbian and illustrates how sexual prejudice serves to maintain women's status in sport.

Organizational Factors

In addition to societal factors, organizational or meso-level factors can also reinforce the lesbian stigma in sport. These factors operate at the group level (e.g., organizational or team level) of analysis and include parents and peers, organizational culture, and leader behaviors.

Parents and peers. Both parents and peers play an instrumental role in shaping one's values and attitudes related to a host of issues (Kandel and Andrews 2009). Generally, children will deviate from traditional gender norms if their parents instill the belief that men and women should have equal opportunities in life (Eccles, Jacobs, and Harold 1990). Research also suggests that parents, especially fathers, tend to encourage boys to pursue activities that require motor skills and discourage girls from partaking in activities that may promote aggressive behaviors (Lytton 2000). Furthermore, research demonstrates how fathers help to shape their children's attitudes toward sport participation in general (Shakib and Dunbar 2004).

Parents' views toward homosexuality can also influence what sports they encourage their children to participate in or what behavior they deem appropriate (Sartore and Cunningham 2009a). Specifically, in regard to the lesbian stigma in sport, girls whose parents do not want them to participate in "masculine" sports (e.g., rugby), or do not want them to play on teams with lesbian teammates or coaches (Ezzell 2009), are often aware of these parental attitudes. The fact that parents do not want their daughters to play with lesbians is particularly evident in Division I women's basketball, to the extent that parents will overtly state this fact during the recruiting process. As such, more coaches now promote their sport programs as "family friendly" as a way to signal to top recruits that they do not have a "lesbian problem" (Cyphers and Fagan 2011).

Whereas family generally molds a person's initial views concerning gender roles and sexuality, peers can strengthen (or mitigate) these beliefs later in life (Kandel and Andrews 2009). This is certainly the case when teammates or coworkers express negative attitudes toward sexual minorities (Melton and Cunningham 2012; Sartore and Cunningham 2010). For instance, a qualitative analysis of lesbian athletes in NCAA Division I basketball (Melton and Cunningham 2012) revealed that teammates who view homosexuality as a sin are often quite vocal and unapologetic when expressing their disapproval of same-sex relationships—causing lesbian teammates to experience feelings of guilt or shame because of their sexual orientation. In the work context, similar dynamics emerge. For example, lesbian employees often conceal their sexual orientation at work to avoid being the subject of negative gossip (Sartore and Cunningham

2010). As is evident by these findings, parents and peers can play a substantial part in fostering lesbian stigma in sport.

Organizational culture. Organizational culture refers to the pattern of shared values, beliefs, and norms that organizational members develop over time (Schein 1990). In most instances, the organization's culture will dictate employee behaviors and serve as a model for newcomers to know what is appropriate conduct in the workplace. Several researchers have examined the impact of culture in regard to diversity and inclusion initiatives in sport organizations (DeSensi 1995; Doherty and Chelladurai 1999; Fink and Pastore 1999). This literature suggests that when diversity is not valued in the workplace, the organization's culture will revolve around the norms and preferences of those who have traditionally held leadership positions in sport organizations—specifically white, heterosexual males.

Recent research of athletic departments illustrates that organizational culture influences the attitudes toward and experiences of women in sport. Interviews with gays and lesbians working in an unsupportive sport environment—meaning that the organization had no formal policies and practices that supported LGBT inclusion, and most employees did not see the value in diversity—provide evidence of this. Though the employees generally expressed high levels of job satisfaction, they acknowledged that lesbian and gay identities were not valued and that they did not always feel comfortable discussing their sexual orientation at work—this was especially the case for lesbian employees. For instance, whereas gay male employees found it easy to gain acceptance in the workplace by emphasizing other social identities (e.g., sport fan, hunter, Republican) they shared with their coworkers, lesbian employees were still expected to present a heterosexual image. In fact, one lesbian employee was told she needed to pretend she had a boyfriend if she wanted to get promoted. Similarly, in another study (Fink et al. 2012), lesbian athletes expressed frustration that their current athletic departments were not more inclusive and felt like it diminished their overall experience. At times, these noninclusive cultures can be so strong that gay and lesbian athletes elect to hide their sexual orientation from most persons in the athletic department (Melton and Cunningham 2012).

Leadership. Leaders can play a central role in perpetuating the lesbian stigma in sport. Their attitudes and behaviors, and the policies they support, establish a model for others to follow in the organization. Social learning theory supports this contention, as Albert

Bandura argued that "virtually all learning phenomena, resulting from direct experience, can occur vicariously by observing other people's behaviors and the consequences for them" (1986:19). Thus, when a leader expresses explicit or implicit negative attitudes toward women, especially those who do not display hyper-feminine traits, it is likely that others in the organization will as well. Consequently, those women who differ from the prototypical majority will continue to be marginalized (Cunningham 2009; Jayne and Dipboye 2004).

These dynamics have been observed in a number of studies in sport (Krane and Barber 2005; Melton 2010a; Melton and Cunningham forthcoming). For instance, a qualitative analysis of lesbian athletes (Melton and Cunningham 2012) found that some coaches displayed overt forms of sexual prejudice. In one shocking example, a coach told a student player that if she did not raise her grades by the end of the semester, he would "pull the gay card" (tell a player's parents that she was gay). Thus, consistent with the notion that sexual prejudice is used to threaten people (Sartore-Baldwin 2012), the coach's hostility permeated throughout the team, and heterosexism took on an institutionalized nature. In this same analysis, dress codes and team policies enforced by the coaching staff revealed more implicit forms of sexual prejudice. For example, some coaches required female players to wear dresses to formal team functions, and it was assumed that only males were allowed to accompany female players to team events where donors and other supporters of the athletic department were in attendance.

Individual Factors

Finally, individual or micro-level factors can also perpetuate the lesbian stigma. These factors relate to the individual level and might represent individual players, coaches, coworkers, and administrators, to name a few. I highlight two micro-level factors here: salient identities and associations with LGBT people.

Identity salience. The social categorization perspective (Tajfel and Turner 1979; Turner et al. 1987) holds that people have multiple identities, such as that of athlete, Latina, woman, daughter, student, lesbian, and the like. Each of these identities can vary in terms of contextual saliency. Thus, a person's sexual orientation may be important in one setting but less significant in others, such that a person's athlete identity might be most salient. However, some people may consider a certain social identity as particularly representative of their self-concept, and consequently this salient identity will influence their thoughts, beliefs, and behaviors across a variety of contexts. For example, some people hold that their religious identity remains salient at all times and greatly influences all of their attitudes and actions, regardless of context.

When predicting if the lesbian stigma will be enacted, it is particularly important to consider the salient identities of heterosexuals and sexual minorities. In regard to heterosexuals' attitudes toward sexual minorities, research suggests that strong identification with religious fundamentalism positively relates to sexual prejudice. Sartore and Cunningham (2010) observed this relationship during their investigation of how the lesbian label serves to stigmatize women in sport organizations. Staff and faculty members who strongly identified as conservative Christians were more likely to endorse heterosexual norms and reject alternate expressions of sexuality. In addition to religious identity, research also shows that individuals who strongly identify as athletes are more likely to exhibit signs of sexual prejudice when their athletic identity is salient to their self-concept (Bush, Anderson, and Carr 2012). Athletes are typically immersed in the sport culture—where prevailing traditions and ideologies privilege masculinity and heterosexuality—so it may not be surprising that these individuals express greater levels of sexual prejudice.

Interestingly, sexual minorities who hold the previously mentioned identities as salient may also be more likely to experience internalized stigma, or self-stigma, and view a society's dominant ideologies as legitimate (see Herek 2009). In a study that examined internalized stigma among sexual minorities, participants manifested higher levels of self-stigma if they affiliated with institutions and ideologies in American society characterized by norms associated with heterosexual masculinity, traditional Christianity, or political conservatism. These findings may explain why heterosexual and lesbian women will sometimes accept, or fail to challenge, gender norms in sport. In sum, these studies highlight the importance of considering how multiple identities may influence attitudes, behaviors, and experiences.

Associations with LGBT people. In the literature on sexual prejudice, empirical investigations consistently demonstrate that the greater number of LGBT friends or acquaintances one has, the less the likelihood that this individual will hold negative attitudes toward sexual minorities (Herek and Capitanio 1996; Pettigrew and Tropp 2006). Indeed, interacting with dissimilar others provides one with the opportunity to learn about the out-group, signifies a behavioral change, allows for affective relationships to form between in-group and out-group members, and reduces stereotypical views of out-group members (Binder et al. 2009; Brown and Hewstone 2005; Pettigrew 1998).

Unfortunately, the very mechanism that can reduce sexual prejudice (contact with LGBT individuals) may also make heterosexual persons vulnerable to stigmatization. According to Gregory Herek (2009), though expressions of sexual prejudice are generally directed toward sexual minorities, some are directed at their friends, family, community members, and allies (i.e., heterosexuals who take a public stand against the discrimination of LGBT individuals). Due to their affiliations with sexual minorities, these individuals experience stigma by association, or what Erving Goffman (1963) terms a "courtesy stigma." Thus, heterosexual athletes or sport employees may face discrimination because they are perceived to be lesbian, or because they support inclusion of lesbians—a view that is not considered popular in women's sport. Consequently, few heterosexual female coaches and players have spoken out in support of lesbians or lesbian rights in the sport context.

Research examining the antecedents of championing diversity also provides support for why heterosexuals may not publicly support inclusion of LGBT people in sport. For instance, Derek Avery (2011) suggests that employees will resist publicly supporting diversity initiatives if they perceive their views are inconsistent with the views of others in the workplace. George Cunningham and Melanie Sartore's (2010) findings support this argument in that employees in their study were less likely to resist diversity, and more likely to champion it, when they believed their coworkers were also strongly committed to diversity. Thus, in order to escape being classified as an out-group member, nonstigmatized individuals (i.e., heterosexuals) may refuse to speak up for LGBT equality and may deliberately distance themselves from sexual minorities.

Consequences of Lesbian Stigma

Minority Stress

Ilan Meyer's (2003) conceptualization of minority stress recognizes that members of stigmatized groups chronically encounter certain stressful events solely because of their devalued position in society.

Accordingly, there are three stress processes that LGBT individuals face. From the most distal to the most proximal, these are stressful occurrences and experiences that affect LBGT individuals because of their sexual orientation (e.g., being verbally or physically attacked), because of their expectations of such events, and because of their internalization of heterosexism and sexual prejudice.

In the sport literature, scholars note that minority stress generally inhibits the physical, psychological, and professional well-being of female athletes (see Sartore and Cunningham 2010). In terms of physical consequences, feeling pressured to meet heterosexual feminine ideals can lead women to adopt a host of unhealthy habits, such as risky sexual behaviors, exercise addiction, substance abuse, or eating disorders (Krane 1997; Krane et al. 2010). Research also suggests women may experience poor psychological health as a result of minority stress. For instance, Vikki Krane (1997) discovered that an unsupportive athletic environment contributed to low self-esteem, low confidence, high stress, and substance abuse among lesbian student-athletes. Similarly, Robert Rotella and Mi Mi Murray (1991) found that negative psychological well-being among LGBT athletes was associated with sexual prejudice and heterosexism they encountered in their respective sports. Furthermore, recent research also demonstrates how the lesbian label stigmatizes athletes of color. Specifically, these athletes experience social isolation, and report having feelings of shame or guilt because of the sexual orientation (Melton and Cunningham 2012).

Identity management techniques. Considering the negative consequences that generally accompany social stigmatization, many women adopt identity management techniques as a way to evade the lesbian stigma and promote a sense of self-worth and affirmation in the sport context. Though there are similarities, identity management strategies can differ based on one's sexual orientation. For gays and lesbians in sport, this usually entails using passing or revealing strategies (Clair, Beatty, and MacLean 2005). Passing is the practice of disguising or withholding one's sexual identity and it can take three forms—fabrication, concealment, or discretion. On the other hand, revealing involves disclosing one's sexual orientation to others. Sexual minorities can reveal their sexual orientation by using signaling, normalizing, or differentiating techniques. In the sport context, research has consistently shown that most lesbian athletes adhere to the norm of silence and subsequently use various strategies to conceal (rather than reveal) their sexual orientation (Griffin 1998; Krane and Barber 2005; Sartore and Cunningham 2009b, 2010).

Considering that the lesbian label is also used to limit the power and opportunities of heterosexual women (Krane 2001; Sartore and Cunningham 2009b, 2010), they too develop a number of coping mechanisms to escape this form of stigmatization. For instance, research suggests that women, particularly when participating in sports that are viewed as more masculine, will engage in "defensive othering"—the process by which members of a subordinate group distance themselves from other subordinates by displaying attitudes and behaviors that reinforce and legitimize their devalued status (Ezzell 2009:111). Specifically, women will take on the views of the dominant group (i.e., emphasizing the notion that men's sport is superior to women's sport, supporting the view that women should not appear too muscular or masculine, or reinforcing the belief that heterosexuality is and should be the norm) in response to the lesbian stigma and backlash that women encounter in sport settings. When relying on this strategy, women cast themselves as the exception to the stereotype, thereby unintentionally reinforcing masculine hegemony and heteronormative ideology in sport. And, while there are differences among lesbians and heterosexual women in terms of how they manage their identity in the sport context, both groups routinely present themselves as ultra-feminine (Krane 2001), or what Griffin (1998) terms "heterosexy," in order to prove their heterosexuality.

Organizational or team performance. Manifestations of minority stress at the individual level (e.g., depression, low self-esteem, low job satisfaction) can also significantly influence group, team, or organizational outcomes. For instance, research suggests that employees who report high levels of work-related stress are more likely to experience poor physical and psychological well-being, which limits their performance at work (Cryer, McCraty, and Childre 2003). However, when employees feel valued and included in the workplace, they are more likely to experience high job satisfaction, which relates to positive organizational outcomes (Milliken and Martins 1996).

Some evidence in the sport literature provides support for this argument. For instance, George Cunningham (2011b) examined performance outcomes related to sexual orientation diversity in NCAA Division I athletic programs. In his study, athletic departments that combined high sexual orientation diversity with a proactive diversity strategy (i.e., a strategy that values diversity and emphasizes inclusion and positively relates to job satisfaction among minorities) were able to significantly outperform other programs—in some instances, these programs achieved almost seven times greater performance than did their peers. In a follow-up study with NCAA Division III athletic departments, findings indicated that high sexual orientation diversity positively related to a creative work environment when the organization had a strong commitment to diversity in general. Of particular interest, the least creative work environments were characterized by high sexual orientation diversity and low commitment to diversity in general. Thus, when an athletic department does not value sexual minorities, it may limit its overall performance.

Potential Moderators

Other factors can of course influence these relationships, three of which I examine here. First, Sartore and Cunningham proposed that the level of stigma consciousness, or "the degree to which women focus on their stereotyped social identity within the sport context" (2010:298), can exacerbate or circumvent the outcomes associated with the lesbian stigma. Thus, women with high levels of stigma consciousness are more likely to anticipate that they will experience negative stereotyping, prejudice, and discrimination. Second, these authors also suggest that the type of sport or job will serve as a moderator. Specifically, women who participate in sports that are viewed as gender-appropriate (i.e., more feminine sports, such as figure skating or gymnastics), or who hold low-status positions, will be more likely to avoid the lesbian stigma than women who participate in sports considered gender-inappropriate (i.e., more masculine sports, such as football or ice hockey), or who occupy high-status positions (e.g., head coach or athletic director) within sport.

Finally, social support may also exaggerate or minimize the possibility that women will experience the lesbian stigma in sport. Social support can provide instrumental, psychological, and physical support (Vaux 1988). Research suggests that minorities who receive support from similar others are less likely to be adversely affected by social stigmatization (Meyer 2003), and this is especially true for sexual minorities (Herek and Garnets 2007). Furthermore, LGBT employees who have supportive coworkers generally report high levels of life satisfaction (Huffman, Watrous-Rodriguez, and King 2008) and feel more comfortable disclosing their sexual orientation in the workplace (Ragins, Singh, and Cornwell 2007). These dynamics have also been observed among athletes and employees in various sport settings (Fink et al. 2012; Melton and Cunningham forthcoming, 2012). Therefore, women who have various forms of social support in sport are less likely to suffer from the consequences associated with the lesbian stigma than those who do not have these resources available to them.

Positive Signs of Change

Although women and sexual minorities have traditionally been relegated to an out-group status in sport, there are still a number of ways they can challenge the legitimacy of the lesbian stigma and promote social change. Specifically, research points to three ways women are proving they can combat dominant norms and ideologies present in sport: creating new definitions of femininity, using social media to break the culture of silence, and forming support groups with athlete allies.

New definitions of femininity. Societal views no longer contend that the female physique need be delicate and dainty. Instead, women are now able to embrace muscularity; however, restricted muscularity is usually valued. Women are no longer afraid to appear athletic, and are less inclined to present themselves in overtly sexualized ways. A recent qualitative analysis by Krane and colleagues (2010) supports this contention. This study revealed that female college athletes from a variety of sports preferred to be photographed in athletic poses so that their athletic identity could be emphasized. Of particular interest, none of the women in the study said that, given the opportunity, they would want to be photographed in a sexualized way. Presenting females in athletic manners also produces positive psychological outcomes. For instance, research suggests that women tend to feel empowered when they see female athletes engaged in their respective sports, and they begin to describe their bodies in terms of what they can do instead of how they appear (Daniels 2009).

Women do not just prefer action photos; they will also protest against media images that focus on femininity instead of athleticism. This became evident as several people voiced complaints when two Division I women's basketball programs (Florida State University and Texas A&M University) produced overtly sexual team posters. Consequently, the following year, the team posters for these two programs depicted the players in their basketball uniforms rather than designer dresses.

Influence of social media. The advent of various forms of social media has given female athletes a way to avert mass media outlets, and has provided them with the opportunity to present themselves to the public in a manner they deem appropriate. Now female athletes can post their own YouTube videos, comment on Facebook or Twitter, or create their own blog without having to answer to gatekeepers in the mass media. Given the infancy of social media, it will be interesting to see if and how this type of communication can help reduce the lesbian stigma in sport.

Athlete allies. Athlete allies also inspire social change in women's sport. Allies are persons, regardless of sexual orientation or gender identity, who take a public a stand against heterosexist practices and sexual prejudice. In sport, athlete ally groups and clubs promote the values of respect, inclusion, and equality in their athletic community. These groups can include competitive and recreational athletes, coaches, teachers, league officials, sport fans, and others involved in sport.

Conclusion

This chapter began with a story of one woman's decision to break the culture of silence and publicly disclose her sexual orientation in sport. Any negative outcomes related to Coach Murrell's decisions are minimal compared to the benefits she gained by being open about who she is and what she values. Unfortunately, in Division I women's basketball, no other women have followed her example, which speaks to the perceived threat and pervasiveness of the lesbian stigma in sport. Though great strides have been made toward gender equality in sport, several influences still serve to legitimize the lesbian stigma and maintain women's subordinate position. Indeed, factors at the societal, organizational, and individual levels lead to a number of negative outcomes by reinforcing the lesbian stigma in sport, including increased minority stress, the felt need to adopt identity management techniques, and poor organizational and team out-comes. Fortunately, women are beginning to actively challenge the dominant ideal of masculinity and heterosexuality in sport. However, greater efforts need to be made by researchers and participants alike in finding ways to rid sport of the lesbian stigma so that everyone, but especially women and sexual minorities, can enjoy athletic com-petition to the fullest.

3

Men, Masculinities, and Sexualities

Eric Anderson, Mark McCormack, and Matt Ripley

Blake's 6-foot 4-inch, 190-pound body shuffled up and down the basketball court as squeaks echoed below him from the wooden floor of his high school gym. Although only a sophomore at the time, Blake drew coverage from local media and praise from his community for being one of the most talented players in Indiana (Anderson 2005a). The rest of his team had gone home, but Blake remained on the court shooting basket after basket.

Although having no dreams of superstardom when he began playing basketball, Blake believed that shooting hoops offered the chance of a college scholarship. However, he wanted this scholarship not just to improve his playing ability but also to escape the confines of the homophobic Midwest: "Basketball is my ticket out of here," Blake said, as he yearned to live in a more liberal, metropolitan city.

Blake first took up basketball unwillingly in the fourth grade, as he sought to raise his social standing among his peers: "I was actually more interested in books, but that's not really cool. I mean I really hated basketball; I'd rather read a book, but other boys didn't do that. Everybody played basketball, and I wanted to fit in, so I did it too" (quoted in Anderson 2005a:77–78). While Blake used basketball to raise his popularity, he also found it a haven from being socially perceived as gay. Realizing that most boys think basketball players *cannot* be gay, Blake used his athletic ability to avoid homophobia.

Blake first began to question his sexuality during sixth grade, and by eighth grade he was certain of what he had feared—that he was gay. "It's not easy to be the thing that all the boys use as a put-down. It's what you call someone when you're trying to diss them, and I certainly did not want to be that!" Accordingly, Blake learned not just how to play basketball but also how to pass as straight. And while the basketball court offered him the safety of heterosexuality, he used the Internet as an arena to explore his same-sex desires.

Blake's confidence began to grow and by the end of his eighth-grade year he ventured out to meet other gay guys. At the end of his freshman year he had even found himself a boyfriend. It was Blake's boyfriend who helped him realize that he was not alone, and that loving another boy was nothing to be ashamed of. "We dated for a few months, which at the age of fourteen seemed like forever, and then one day he just stopped calling. I couldn't figure out why he wasn't returning my calls or e-mails."

Being closeted, Blake had no adult to express his anguish to, and so he dealt with these feelings of rejection by venting online. "I was talking to a friend, asking if he had heard from Chris." His friend replied, "Didn't you hear? Chris was killed in a car accident." "I started to cry. So I ran to the bathroom and turned the radio up as loud as it went so nobody could hear me" (quoted in Anderson 2005a:78). Life in the closet meant Blake had no one to comfort him during his anguish.

Interviewed in the late 1990s, Blake cut a sad figure at the time. While he walked the hallways of his rural high school as publicly popular, he was emotionally alienated. Blake was also daunted by the insistent fear of being discovered as gay: "I fear all the time that others will find out. That people's opinions of me will change if they find out that I'm gay. Like my teachers, they won't think the same of me; they make gay comments and say them in a derogatory manner. Even my little bro will say stuff about gay people. It makes it hard, I'm always thinking in the back of my mind, *would you feel this way about me if you knew I was gay?*" (quoted in Anderson 2005a:79). Compounding matters, Blake feared that his parents suspected he was gay. "They don't want to talk about it. Mom says, 'Blake you need to get a girlfriend.' 'Mom I don't want to,' I tell her. 'I don't have time. I'm too busy. I have to get my workout in'" (quoted in Anderson, 2005a:80). It was here that basketball became the all-purpose excuse for Blake, not only providing him with a veneer of heterosexuality, but also giving him something to do other than date women.

Connecting Sport with Homophobia

Blake's story was typical for the majority of men throughout the 1980s and 1990s. They feared coming out and thus resorted to passing as heterosexual in order to avoid the emotional and often violent hostility toward gays and lesbians (Anderson 2005a; Griffin 1998). This level of fear was no more prominent than in sport, where homophobia was a required attitude (Pronger 1990). This is evidenced by the tiny presence of openly gay athletes over the past three decades (Anderson 2011a).

The realm of sport has not only traditionally rejected homosexuality but also venerated hyper-heterosexuality (Griffin 1998; Hekma 1998; Pronger 1990). The question that sport and gender scholars have studied over the past three decades is why sport, and sporting *men* in particular, have placed such value in homophobia and sexual prejudice.

Much of our cultural obsession with competitive team sport originated at the beginning of the twentieth century. At that time, there was a fear that men were "going soft" (Anderson 2009). With Western societies shifting from primarily agrarian ones to countries where the majority of the population lived in cities, the social structure of work changed significantly. In the new urban life, instead of working as a family on the farm, men worked in factories, structuring away from their families and leaving women to care for the children (Hartmann 1976). The social effect of this may have been better limited were it not for the work of Sigmund Freud (see Anderson 2009).

Freud noticed that city-dwelling resulted in elevated rates of same-sex sexual activity. Rather than attributing this to the increased chances of men with similar desires being able to meet (the sociological explanation), he instead attributed it to the separation of children from male role models. Homosexuality, for Freud, was not an innate sexual desire; it was an inversion, a form of gendered wrongdoing. While Freud's theories have been categorically disproved (LeVay 2010), they carried cultural weight at the time and sent a largely homophobic population into moral panic.

It was at that time that sport became organized and culturally valued. Freud had highlighted a problem—that boys did not have enough male influence—and sport provided the answer: time in the company of a coach, a male role model who could provide the requisite male (and moral) vapors. Accordingly, sports like rugby and football were valued, as they provided sufficient masculinity for these feminized boys (Anderson and McCormack 2010a, 2010b; Chandler and Nauright 1996).

There were other reasons that team sports were valued for boys. For example, sport helped teach the values of self-sacrifice and obedience to authority needed in both factory work and the military. However, the key factor was that sport accentuated the extreme version of masculinity that Western culture demanded. This is why women were excluded from sport for so long: women who competed equally alongside men would disrupt the myth of men's athleticism and women's frailty (Burton-Nelson 1995).

The homophobia of sport served to stratify men according to a hierarchical ranking of masculinities (see Connell 1995), with homophobia the key mechanism for regulating men (Pronger 1990). This became most serious in the 1980s, a time that was the most homohysteric (a culture of heightened awareness that homosexuality exists among its population, and of elevated homophobia) in modern history (Anderson 2009). There were three reasons for this.

First, increasing fundamentalist religiosity brought a religious backlash from the Christian churches, which stirred up hatred against the homosexual community in an attempt to both "cleanse" the nation and also increase financial revenue through greater donations. Second, this fundamentalism was tangled (particularly in the United States) with conservative politics: President Ronald Reagan was not just an ex–movie star cowboy but also represented the party of God (Peterson 2011). Finally, homosexuality was associated with HIV/AIDS, which ripped through the gay community killing tens of thousands. The combination of these three events led to high levels of homophobia; thus men went to great lengths to avoid being socially perceived as gay (Peterson and Anderson 2012).

Decreasing Cultural Homophobia and Sexual Prejudice

Social attitudes toward homosexuality began to transition in the 1990s, with large-scale quantitative research documenting significant improvements during this time (Loftus 2001). However, homophobia remained a problem during this period, and qualitative studies reported that heterosexual athletes were still espousing homophobic attitudes (Hekma 1998). During this time, Lisa Wolf Wendel, J. Douglas Toma, and Christopher Morphew wrote: "Examining the overall message from these results, we found hostility to gay men and lesbians on nearly all teams and at all case study sites. Clearly those from intercollegiate level athletics are generally unwilling to confront and accept homosexuality" (2001:470). Gay athletes therefore remained closeted, as the social sanctions for coming out were too great. This made studying openly gay athletes impossible. For example, in his 1990 work on the subject, Brian Pronger only studied closeted gay male athletes.

It was not until the turn of the millennium that gay athletes began coming out in significant numbers, mostly at the high school and university level of play. In 2002, Eric Anderson published the first research on the experiences of openly gay male athletes (twenty-six individuals, aged eighteen to twenty-five). In his qualitative study, he identified how orthodox notions of masculinity (men as macho, heterosexual, aggressive, and stoic) were not seamless—that the presence of gay male athletes, especially those who had as much or better athletic ability than heterosexual athletes, challenged hegemonic notions of masculinity. He found that despite the fact that gay male athletes were culturally silenced, there was a near-total absence of physical and verbal abuse against these athletes. However, Anderson found that gay athletes were only accepted if they were valuable to the mantra of athletics—winning.

Anderson found that most of the athletes he interviewed were unexpectedly pleased with their coming-out experience. Indeed, most of the athletes suggested that they wished they had come out sooner. He also found gay athletes praising their coaches and teammates for their liberal attitudes and acceptance.

However, these participants also discussed less positive experiences, the significance of which they minimized. For example, one of the participants, Gabriel, initially spoke of his coming-out experience in glowing terms. With two openly gay teammates already, he said that his overall experience was "very good." He even praised his coach and teammates for their support: "The first people I came out to were actually runners, and my coach. I went to a private school and one day we were sitting around talking . . . and a runner came out to us . . . so I did too. . . . From then, I was able to open up to the other runners. . . . And no one really had a problem or an issue with the fact that we were gay" (quoted in Anderson 2002:867). Gabriel went on to tell Anderson about his 1600-meter relay race in the state finals: "My friend [also openly gay] and I were approached by our other two [heterosexual] teammates right before the final race. They reached into their bags and pulled out two gay pride socks and said that they wanted to wear them. We were really touched. And they pulled out two more pairs and said they were going to wear them in support of us" (867).

Gabriel remembered these events vividly and used them to summarize his experiences more generally. But when asked for a more detailed account of his initial coming out, he recalled that there were some problems. Contradicting his earlier statement, he indicated that he had lost a friend when word spread about his sexuality: "We were at camp, and we had been around these guys for year, and someone had found out that we were gay and had a fit over it. I was kind of hurt by it. Certain things that were said were out of place. This individual completely left the camp and did not run that year because of what his friends would think because he was running with us. . . . I'd say he was one of our good friends . . . he no longer spoke to me" (867).

Anderson (2002) found numerous accounts of athletes speaking of their experiences as positive, praising teammates and talking about how accepted they felt while at the same time speaking about heterosexist thinking, the silencing of sexual desire, and the frequent use of homophobic language. Even when the inequality was highlighted, these athletes still did not seem to feel the impact of having been discriminated against. Anderson theorized this blindness to discrimination as being a form of reverse relative deprivation. Relative deprivation theory states that people compare their situation with that of those who have things better and, in doing so, view their situation as overly negative (Davies 1962; Tilly 1978). However, these gay athletes were doing the reverse of this—overemphasizing the positives of their experiences because they had expected their situation to be so much worse (Anderson 2005a).

Don't Ask, Don't Tell

One of the more persistent forms of discrimination that athletes encountered in Anderson's (2002) study was the silencing of their sexual desires and sexual activities. Effectively living segmented identities, the sporting form of "don't ask, don't tell" accepted gay athletes but prohibited discussion of their sexual identity afterward. For example, Tim, an openly gay tennis player, said he was not treated any differently after coming out: "They didn't really treat me as gay. In fact they didn't even mention it really. They just treated me like one of the guys and stuff. Sorta like nothing changed." He was then asked if this included verbally sexualizing women. "Yeah, they ask me like who I think is hot and stuff." But Tim commented that they would never discuss which men he found attractive: "They'd never do that. They don't want to hear that kind of stuff" (quoted in Anderson 2002:870).

Gay athletes of this time often failed to recognize that their identities were being denied, and they often took part in their own oppression by self-silencing and partaking in heterosexual dialogue. Whereas their teammates proudly boasted of their heterosexual exploits, the gay athletes did not discuss their same-sex activities. However, victimized by a culture that resisted discourse on same-sex desire, gay athletes often viewed their silencing as acceptable, and embodied a segmented identity that contributed to their own culture of silence (Hekma 1998). As Dana Britton and Christine Williams (1995) argued that with the military (before the ban on gay soldiers), such a culture reflects the institutional and cultural privileging of a heterosexual masculine ideal.

Policies such as "don't ask, don't tell," whether official or not, highlight that the social regulation of acceptable topics of discussion is a powerful form of heterosexual hegemony. In the absence of the ability to ban openly gay athletes from sport, heterosexual athletes resisted the intrusion of gay athletes through the creation of a culture of silence. The combined effect of the attempted silencing of gay identities within sport, and the willful promotion of heterosexuality, served to privilege heterosexuality while marginalizing homosexuality, and prevented the association of homosexuality as being compatible with sport.

Homophobic Language

Men have traditionally consolidated a heterosexual identity and masculine standing by overtly discriminating against homosexuality through the use of homophobic language (Plummer 1999). Through the use of homophobic language, male behaviors are regulated and men avoid any connotation with femininity or homosexuality. Consequently, this has limited male expressions of gender and sexuality (Pronger 1990), and has been a key factor in the unwillingness of gay athletes to come out of the closet.

However, Anderson found that homophobic language was not necessarily indicative of anti-gay sentiment. For example, Frank, an openly gay football player, told him that he was surprised at how well he was received on his team, because his teammates had used such a high degree of homophobic language before he came out: "I couldn't believe how cool the guys were with me. I mean I expected them to be really un-accepting of me because they'd called me a fag for so long. I mean, they call everyone a fag, so it's not like they thought I was gay or anything, but still I thought that when they found out I really was, you know gay, that they'd hate me" (quoted in Anderson 2002:871). When asked if they still called him a fag now that he had come out, he responded, "No. Not really. I mean, every now and then they might say it, but they usually apologize and say that they didn't mean it that way" (871). This links with scholars' recognition that homophobia is often concerned with regulating gender rather than sexuality (see Kimmel 1994).

But despite the attempts of some of their teammates to reduce homophobic language through use of the word "fag," most of Anderson's openly gay interviewees reported much less sensitivity toward their teammates' use of the word "gay." Frank said, "Oh yeah, they say everything is gay if they don't like it. I mean, if you're being dumb, they say, 'don't be gay,' and if your team was given a penalty unfairly they say, 'that's so gay'" (872). Similarly, Ken said, "They say, 'this is gay,' and 'that's gay,' but they don't mean it like that" (872), even though Ken reported not using the word in such manner himself. In fact, none of the informants strongly objected to the use of the word "gay" by their teammates to describe things they deemed distasteful, even though they didn't use the word in such manner themselves.

Anderson's (2002) findings were consistent with those of Gert Hekma (1998) and Michael Price (2000), who both found that gay athletes frequently heard anti-gay language spoken by their heterosexual teammates and opponents, but did not necessarily attribute this to anti-gay sentiment. Price argued that homophobic language takes on a significantly different meaning in sport, as it appeared to be an accepted element of athletic competition. However, Hekma argued that the frequency of anti-gay language meant that gay athletes dismissed it as habitual rather than indicative of anti-gay views.

In support of Hekma's (1998) findings, many of the openly gay athletes Anderson interviewed did not seem to take offense at the use of the words "fag" or "gay," by saying "they didn't mean it that way." However, unlike Hekma's findings, not all athletes in Anderson's research dismissed the hostile capacity of such language.

Specifically, many of the closeted athletes felt that it created a hostile environment, and they used such language to gauge the level of comfort their teams maintained toward homosexuality.

Most of the closeted athletes whom Anderson interviewed reported to him that one of the reasons they had not come out was because they perceived their teammates as being highly homophobic as evidenced by homophobic language. Jon, a closeted high school football player, described his sport as "the most homophobic" by saying that "everything was fag this and fag that" (quoted in Anderson 2002:872). And one openly gay interviewee said that before he came out, he feared doing so because of the degree of homophobic language he heard on his team: "I was totally afraid to come out to my teammates, I mean they are always calling other people fags and stuff" (872).

Openly Gay Athletes Today

There has been a paucity of research on openly gay male athletes since Anderson's original study. Addressing this concern, Anderson replicated his original study, locating new participants through Internet searches and snowball sampling, and found signs of positive change (Anderson 2011b). His 2002 and 2011 studies enable a comparison to be made that demonstrates significant positive changes. For example, in the 2002 research, all the athletes Anderson interviewed (who were located through the same methods used in the 2011 research) heard frequent use of the word "fag" and phrases such as "that's so gay." However, athletes in the 2011 study heard it less often, and many of them reported that these words and phrases were not used at all. Furthermore, athletes in the 2011 research who did hear such language interpreted it differently.

In 2002, Anderson determined that half of the athletes he interviewed judged levels of homophobia on their sport teams through the amount of homophobic language their teammates used. This half of the 2002 sample argued that the term "that's gay" and the use of the word "fag" were indicative of homophobic attitudes among those who used them; the other half argued that this was not the case. In the 2011 sample, however, athletes did not judge the level of their teammates' homophobia through the use of this language. Neil explained: "Gay doesn't mean gay anymore. And fag doesn't' mean fag. You can't say that because someone says 'that's so gay' or 'he's a fag' that they are homophobic. I guess they could be, but you know when someone is using those words as a homophobic insult and when someone's not" (quoted in Anderson 2011b:258). Like Neil, and in contrast to the 2002 sample, all the athletes in the 2011 sample who heard use of the words "gay" and "fag" argued that these phrases were not homophobic. Supporting this, scholars have argued that the reason athletes and others dismiss these terms as homophobic insults is that the social context of this language use has changed (Lalor and Rendle-Short 2007; McCormack 2012; McCormack and Anderson 2010b).

Positive Discussions About Homosexuality

The improved experience of those in Anderson's 2011 cohort compared to those in the 2002 cohort is also evidenced by the manner in which the gay athletes discussed homosexuality with their teammates. All but two evaded the culture of "don't ask, don't tell" that Anderson found in half of the athletes he interviewed in his first study. For example, in 2002, Anderson argued:

> In the absence of the ability to ban openly gay athletes from sport, heterosexual athletes within team sports, both contact and non-contact, resisted the intrusion of openly gay athletes through the creation of a culture of silence around gay identities. Although publicly out, the informants in this study were victimized by heterosexual hegemony and largely maintained a heteronormative framework by self-silencing their speech, and frequently engaged in heterosexual dialogue with their heterosexual teammates. (874)

However, the gay athletes in the 2011 sample told Anderson that their heterosexual teammates discussed issues of homosexuality and gay life openly. The gay athletes were asked about the "types" of guys they liked, and even asked about which teammates they thought were attractive. "Of course we talk about my sexuality," Mark said. "We talk about it all the time." He added: "I think it's fair to say that I'm known as 'the gay hockey player' at my high school. I'm the only gay athlete who is out, even though I suspect a few more. . . . It's funny, I'll be at a party, and meet someone new and they will be like, 'hey, I heard of you. You're the gay hockey player, huh?'" (quoted in Anderson 2011b:260). Anderson asked Mark what type of reception he received after having these start-up conversations. "Oh,

it's always something positive. Like, 'that's cool, man' or whatever.
. . . No I never have a problem. . . . In fact my teammates will sometimes introduce me as their gay friend" (260).

However, Joey, an openly gay wrestler at his high school in a
state known for its religious conservatism, said that while he had no
difficulties, even with his fundamentalist teammates, not all of them
talked about his sexuality. "Yeah, they all know. It's just not a big
deal." But Joey added: "I try not to make a big deal about it . . . there
are a lot of [religious guys] on my team, and they never say anything
about it, but at the same time I try not to put it in their faces. . . .
Other guys on the team talk about it, but I just think that it's an interesting mix of people on the team. So yeah, some of the guys talk
about it with me, and like sometimes we make jokes when practicing,
but the [religious] guys don't so much" (261).

Anderson asked Joey if he ever encountered difficulties when the
more conservative boys had to wrestle with him in practice. "No," he
said. "They just wrestle me. It's not an issue, really. They are still my
friends, we still hang out together after practice, but we don't really
discuss my sexuality much" (261). Joey's statement reflects the type
of "don't ask, don't tell" narratives that existed among half of the gay
athletes in Anderson's 2002 research, and in this case it might also
reflect a strategy to avoid discussing the potentially uncomfortable
topic about whether Joey is aroused when he grapples with the bodies of other fit male athletes.

However, among these gay athletes, Joey was an outlier; the rest
did talk about their sexuality to their teammates. Tim, for example,
said that his swimming teammates joked about his sexuality all the
time: "They love it. I mean do you have any idea how much shit I get
for it? Not like bad stuff, I mean, it's always guys pretending to be
interested in fucking me, or guys bending over in front of me. That
sort of thing. They laugh, I laugh. Everybody just has fun with it. It's
like, we joke about it, daily" (261).

Nullifying Athletic Capital

In 2002, Anderson found that most of the twenty-six openly gay athletes he interviewed were highly accomplished sportsmen, often the
best on their teams. He argued that they used this sporting capital to
dispel the potential stigma associated with being gay. Notably, the
athletes in the 2011 sample did not all possess the same high levels
of status on their respective teams. Of the twenty-six gay athletes An-

derson interviewed in 2011, only six reported being among the top athletes on their teams; most described their athletic performances as average within their team.

For example, Joey said, "I'm a good wrestler, but certainly not the best." John, a university swimmer, maintained that his ability had nothing to do with his positive experience of being openly gay: "Maybe being better would be good, but not because I think my teammates would be any cooler with it. I think it would just be more fun." Unlike Joey and John, Mark was one of the top players on his high school hockey team: "Yeah, I'm good. But that's not why my teammates accept me. They accept me because I'm Mark. I don't think my skills have much to do with it. They liked me before I came out, why wouldn't they like me now?" (quoted in Anderson 2011b:261). While it may be the case that athletic capital matters in homophobic settings, for the athletes in the 2011 sample it was not a variable of importance. Their positive experiences were largely independent of athletic abilities.

Social Support

The homosocial bond between members of sports teams bridges many arenas of their social lives. Teammates often spend large parts of their days together practicing, attending school, and (in the case of most collegiate and professional athletes) living together, in what is a near-total institution (Anderson 2010). This has traditionally created a rigid and tightly controlled bond between team members in accordance with the mandates of hegemonic masculinity. Accordingly, in Anderson's 2002 research, he stressed that, in this narrow social world of hyper-heterosexuality and hyper-masculinity, the presence of an openly gay male athlete creates dissonance where there was once masculine homogeneity. Gay athletes remind their teams that athleticism does not necessarily imply heterosexuality—a threat to the archetypal jock figure. Gay athletes would often lead segmented lives—being out to friends but not teammates.

However, for the athletes in Anderson's 2011 sample, being out to one's peers was the same as being out to one's teammates. It was their perception that their teammates were not more homophobic than nonathletes, and that there was not a clique or cluster of homophobic athletes at their school, that allowed these men to be open about their sexual identity. For example, one of Anderson's 2011 interviewees, Neil, found that when he came out, it actually drew him closer to his teammates. However, he did have difficulties with adults. One of the athletic directors asked him, "Why don't you just choose to be straight?" Neil told Anderson that it was "only adults" who had a hard time with his sexuality (quoted in Anderson 2011b:263).

Grant had support from his friends, too. Yet, like many others, Grant feared coming out to his parents: "My dad is a major homophobe." He added: "He's always bitching about my gay uncle. He says things like, 'Bob is making an issue out of things.' He won't say it in person, but after he leaves he does. It's really awkward and uncomfortable. . . . I have to be careful that when my friends come over they don't say anything" (263). Joey attributed his teammates' silence about his sexuality to their parents, as a result of their parents' homophobia: "I don't think they have a problem with it, actually. I think they don't want their parents to know because *they* will have a problem with it!" (263).

Accordingly, there was often a real disconnect between many of these young gay men and at least some of the adults in their lives. John said, "It's a whole different thing coming out to old people. Some will be fine with it I'm sure, but like is it really worth it? They are from a generation who just doesn't get it" (264). Thus, from the perspective of the athletes whom Anderson interviewed in his 2011 research, decreasing homophobia was an uneven social phenomenon that differed across the generations.

The gay athletes from Anderson's 2011 sample did not fear coming out in the same way or to the same degree as the athletes from his 2002 sample (both samples represented the same class and racial demographic). Unlike the latter, the athletes from the 2011 sample did not fear that their coming out would result in physical hostility, marginalization, or social exclusion (either on or off the field).

Relating Decreasing Homophobia in Sport to Masculinities

This chapter has thus far highlighted that homophobia in sport is not just an artifact of a broader homophobic culture, but that the realm of sport was esteemed precisely because of its ability to privilege heterosexuality. The intersection of homophobia with masculinity in sport is significant. In order to understand why the decrease in homophobia has occurred so rapidly in sport, it is necessary to theorize the social ordering of masculinities.

The most prominent theoretical tool for understanding the social stratification of masculinities has been Raewyn Connell's (1995) concept of hegemonic masculinity. From a social constructionist perspective, hegemonic masculinity theory articulates two social processes. The first concerns how all men benefit from patriarchy. Connell describes hegemonic masculinity as a configuration of gender practices that embody the currently accepted answer to the problem of patriarchy. The second process concerns the mechanisms by which an intra-masculine hierarchy is created and legitimized. Connell argues that these two processes work simultaneously to produce a gender order—one in which certain men are privileged over other men and all men maintain power over all women.

In conceptualizing intra-masculine domination, Connell argues that one archetype of masculinity is esteemed above all others, so that boys and men who most closely embody this standard are accorded the most social capital. Gay men are at the bottom of the hierarchy, and straight men who behave in ways that conflict with this valorized masculinity are marginalized. Accordingly, in this model, homophobia is a particularly effective weapon to stratify men in deference to a hegemonic mode of heteromasculine dominance.

While this has been a model with great utility, hegemonic masculinity fails to accurately account for what occurs in a macro or local culture of *decreased* cultural homophobia. Furthermore, the model permits only one form of masculinity to reside at the top of a social hierarchy; it does not explain the social processes in an environment in which multiple versions of masculinity have equal appeal (McCormack 2011b). In their reformulation of hegemonic masculinity, Connell and James Messerschmidt (2005) reaffirm that hegemonic masculinity presupposes the subordination of nonhegemonic masculinities, and that it is predicated upon *one* dominating (hegemonic) archetype of masculinity. While the attributes of this archetype can change, an essential component is that other masculinities will be hierarchically stratified in relation to it. Accordingly, the theory of hegemonic masculinity is incapable of explaining empirical research that documents multiple masculinities of equal cultural value (Anderson 2005b; McCormack 2011a).

The inability to conceptualize varying masculinities in a culture of decreased homophobia arises from the fact that Connell's work has a limited engagement with hegemony theory (McCormack 2012). Whereas Antonio Gramsci (1971) allowed for aspirational and positive forms of hegemony to prosper (Williams 1977), Connell's use of hegemony theory does not allow for positive hegemony to occur (Beasley 2008; Howson 2006; McCormack 2012).

This was not an issue in the 1980s, when Connell developed her work, or the 1990s, when it was widely taken up in the literature—a highly homophobic period of time, when gay men faced extreme social marginalization (Pronger 1990). However, the inability of Connell's theory to recognize positive forms of hegemony became increasingly problematic as homophobia began to decrease (McCormack and Anderson 2010a, 2010b; Savin-Williams 2005; Weeks 2007). With the decrease in cultural homophobia, hegemonic masculinity theory simply could not account for the varying masculinities that researchers found flourishing without hierarchy or hegemony in many settings (Anderson 2009; McCormack 2011a). Anderson (2005b, 2009) developed inclusive masculinity theory to provide a theoretical explanation of these changes.

Inclusive masculinity theory (Anderson 2009) situates hegemonic masculinity theory in its historical context. It does this through the concept of homohysteria. This is defined as the fear men maintain of being socially perceived as gay. Whereas homophobia is the dislike of homosexuality, a culture is homohysteric when men fear that they will be perceived as gay through the wrongdoing of gendered behaviors.

Anderson (2009) argues that Connell's theory is valid only in periods of high homohysteria. In these times, boys and men are compelled to express homophobic and sexist attitudes, to raise their masculine capital through sport and muscularity, and to raise their heterosexual capital through the public and explicit sexual objectification of women. They also avoid emotional intimacy or homosocial touch. All of this is to escape the stigma of being considered gay (Anderson 2008b). It is within this cultural context that Kimmel (1994) suggests masculinity *as* homophobia.

However, inclusive masculinity theory maintains that as homohysteria declines, multiple masculinities can be *equally* esteemed. This is an important theoretical difference: inclusive masculinity theory situates hegemonic masculinity as the product of homohysteric cultures and enables the understanding of a horizontal alignment of masculinities in settings where men do not fear being labeled as homosexual. With hegemonic masculinity theory there is always a hierarchical stratification of masculinities, and archetypes of masculinity cannot exist without struggle between them. In a culture of inclusive masculinity, however, not only will multiple masculinities coexist harmoniously, but fewer behaviors will be negatively associated with homosexuality.

Inclusive masculinity theory supersedes hegemonic masculinity in explaining the stratification of men because, as well as being a more adaptable heuristic tool, it is able to explain the social dynamics of masculinities in times of lower homohysteria. In inclusive settings with low homohysteria, heterosexual boys and men are permitted to engage in an increasing range of behaviors that once led to homosexual suspicion, all without threat to their publicly perceived heterosexual identities.

For example, fraternity members (Anderson 2008b), rugby players (Anderson and McGuire 2010), school boys (McCormack and Anderson 2010a), heterosexual cheerleaders (Anderson 2008a), and even the men of a Catholic college soccer team in the Midwest (Anderson forthcoming) have been shown to maintain close physical and emotional relationships with each other. Indeed, Mark McCormack (2012) shows that among English high school students at three different schools in the United Kingdom (lower, middle, and upper-middle class), young men express physical touch, and homophobia (including homophobic language) is stigmatized.

While these studies point to positive developments in the organization and stratification of men in particular institutions, homohysteria is decreasing (although not uniformly) across educationally based sport teams in the United States and the United Kingdom. In ethnographic investigations of undergraduate sport teams, spread across both the United States and the United Kingdom, attitudes toward homosexuality have been shown to be positive among heterosexual teammates even though heterosexism often persists (Anderson 2008a; Adams and Anderson forthcoming; Adams, Anderson, and McCormack 2010).

In Anderson's (2009) explication of inclusive masculinity theory, he theorized that this cultural shift, from homophobia to a stigmatization of homophobia, was due to multiple influences: the Internet, the media, decreasing cultural religiosity, the success of feminism, the success of gay and lesbian social politics, and the influence of the increased numbers of gays and lesbians coming out. Interestingly, in the realm of gay male athletes, these changes have frequently occurred against the desires of their coaches or other influential males (Adams, Anderson, and McCormack 2010; McCormack and Anderson 2010b).

Complicating Understandings of Homosexually Themed Language

As previously discussed, there has been a rapid decrease in homophobia within sport settings (Anderson 2011a; Anderson and McGuire 2010). An important addition to the literature on homophobia in sport settings was Mark McCormack's (2011c) conceptual mapping of the use of homophobic language, and what he calls homosexually themed language. Previously, discussions of language use had tended to remain fixated on whether a particular word or phrase was homophobic or not. Yet this simplification obscured the complex nature of homosexually themed language, as it conflated intent and impact and failed to engage with the range of verbal practices that have some form of homosexual content.

It is vital to understand the meanings and dynamics of language because it is the currency through which ideas and social norms are reproduced (Cameron and Kulick 2003; Kiesling 2007). Eric Anderson (2002) demonstrates how the prevalence of homophobic language has been instrumental in many gay athletes' decisions to remain closeted, because these athletes have viewed homophobic language as indicative of a hostile climate toward sexual minorities. However, more recent research documents less damaging forms of homosexually themed language in sport settings and even suggests that it can have positive social effects (McCormack and Anderson 2010b). Accordingly, McCormack (2011c) argued that it is necessary to explore the multiple meanings of homophobic and homosexually themed language in order to understand the regulation and stratification of sexuality within sport as well as in the wider culture. And although there is a diverse body of literature on the topic (McCormack and Anderson 2010b; Pascoe 2005; Rasmussen 2004), understandings are all too frequently based on a simplistic conceptualization of whether language is or is not homophobic.

Merely focusing on the frequency of usage of homophobic language is problematic because it can lead to an exaggeration of the prevalence of homophobia. This is because many people have been socialized into a culture where almost all colloquial language relating to homosexuality has been homophobic, making people at risk of hearing homophobia in language whether it is there or not (McCormack 2011c). This is problematic because fear of homophobia (even when this fear is unwarranted) can cause gay people to remain closeted (Anderson 2002). In order to clarify what homophobic language consists of, McCormack (2011c) argues that the literature documents two requisite features: it is said with pernicious intent, and it has a negative social effect.

The first requirement of homophobic language, pernicious intent, is present when the speaker intends to marginalize a person or act by use of the association with homosexuality. Crispin Thurlow (2001) evidenced the importance of intent by examining "intensifiers"—additional words that demonstrate a desire to wound a person. In this manner, a person would say "you fucking queer" rather than "you queer." Significantly, Thurlow found that intensifiers were used more frequently with anti-gay epithets than any other form of abuse.

McCormack (2011c) describes the second component of homophobic language, as traditionally conceived, as the presence of a negative social effect. Evidencing this, the emotional trauma of homophobic bullying in youth is a frequent narrative of lesbian and gay adults (Flowers and Buston 2001; Plummer 1999). Furthermore, research also highlights the negative social impact this has on students and athletes, including social isolation, school absenteeism, and higher dropout rates in school (Warwick, Aggleton, and Douglas 2001), as well as lower rates of sport participation and ostracization within sport teams (Brackenridge et al. 2008; Pronger 1990).

When McCormack (2011c) conceptualized homophobic language, he highlighted that scholars had in fact conflated the importance of the local culture into the importance of intent. That is, it is implicit in most research that this homophobic language is said within a homophobic environment. The assumption of a homophobic environment is understandable given that the vast majority of the research on homophobic language occurred between 1980 and 2000, when British and American cultures were homophobic. Eric Anderson (2009) and Jeni Loftus (2001) use General Social Survey data to make this point, and Anderson (2009) adds the British Social Attitudes survey to further evidence changing attitudes. This marked decrease in levels of homophobia of recent years necessitates that this assumption be made explicit, for the cultural context to be recognized. Accordingly, McCormack (2011c) proposed an additional factor for analyzing homophobic language—not just intent or effect—but also a homophobic environment.

This linking of environment with effect and intent helps to historically contextualize the conceptualization of homophobic language that so accurately captured the social dynamics of the 1980s and early 1990s (see Anderson 2005b; Griffin 1998; Plummer 1999). However, some scholars continue to argue that the phrase "that's so gay" is homophobic despite decreasing cultural homophobia (see De-Palma and Jennett 2010). Yet they do this without critical investigation of the attitudes of those using the language and what their intent is with the discourse. As a result, they tend to misattribute the phrase as homophobic because they do not engage with attitudes toward homosexuality. Equally problematic, they tend not to engage with how students interpret this language and the effect it has on those receiving it (notable exceptions are Adams, Anderson, and McCormack 2010 and Lalor and Rendle-Short 2007).

Understandings of homosexually themed language were somewhat complicated by C. J. Pascoe's (2005) notion of "fag discourse." This conceptualized a gendered form of homophobia that did not necessarily intend to stigmatize same-sex desire. For example, Pascoe highlighted that "some boys took pains to say that 'fag' is not about sexuality" (2005:336). Fag discourse conceptualizes the use of anti-gay epithets that come from antipathy toward gender nonconformity, not homosexuality. However, she did not link this with the decreasing homophobia that was evident in her ethnography.

Conceptualizing Gay Language

While other scholars discussed the changing nature of homosexually themed language (Lalor and Rendle-Short 2007; Rasmussen 2004), McCormack and Anderson (2010b) were the first to conceptualize this changing form with respect to decreasing homophobia. Here they employed William Ogburn's (1950) concept of cultural lag to understand the phrase "don't be gay."

Cultural lag occurs when two related social variables become dissociated because the meanings change at different rates. In this case, adolescents employ this language without consideration or even knowledge of what it once conveyed. McCormack and Anderson (2010b) found that athletes' use of language lagged behind their pro-gay attitudes. Accordingly, they developed a new way of understanding youths' use of this language, one that did not position the participants as implicit homophobes. As McCormack (2011c) discussed, their concept, which they called gay discourse, ameliorated this issue by positing that the language, while implicitly privileging heterosexuality, did not have the negative social effects of either homophobic language or fag discourse. With a more inclusive environment and an absence of pernicious intent, the social effects of this language are far less negative.

In order to understand the limited extent of this negative effect, it is important to recognize that the word "gay" has been used in many contemporary youth settings as an expression of displeasure without intent to reflect or transmit homophobia (Adams, Anderson, and Mc-Cormack 2010; Lalor and Rendle-Short 2007; McCormack 2011a; McCormack and Anderson 2010a). This means that when young people hear the word "gay" used negatively, they do not automatically associate it with homosexuality, and it is not necessarily the case that the expression of dissatisfaction translates to negative feelings about same-sex desires or gay people.

The lack of negative social effect has been examined within adolescent sport cultures. As discussed earlier, Anderson's (2011b) most recent examination of the experiences of openly gay male athletes finds that they do not attribute anti-gay sentiment to the phrase "that's so gay." Indeed, one of his respondents argued that "you can't judge homophobia that way. . . . The word has different meanings and most of the time it's not got anything to do with gay" (2011b:260). Furthermore, all of his participants argued that use of the words "gay" and "fag" was not indicative of homophobia. They also did not use the prevalence of the word as a determining factor when deciding to come out. Accordingly, the negativity from the use of homosexually themed language has been expunged in these instances.

McCormack (2011c) argued that these findings demonstrate the importance of foregrounding the pivotal role that cultural context has in discerning the intent, interpretations, and social effects of language. This has the implication that no phrase or words are *necessarily* homophobic (nor, indeed, pro-gay). For example, closeted gay athletes in the 1980s and early 1990s would have frequently heard the phrase "that's so gay" and interpreted it as deeply homophobic, which would have had ultimately negative effects on them. However, these athletes were living in the homophobic sport culture of the 1980s and early 1990s, when the phrase "that's so gay" was heard alongside homophobic pejoratives such as "poof," "shirtlifter," and "queer" (in the United Kingdom) and "fag" (in the United States). Athletes in the same sports today, however, experience a different culture, as homophobia has rapidly declined (Anderson 2002, 2011a). Consequently, gay athletes today interpret the phrase "that's so gay" very differently than it was interpreted in the past. The point is that the categorization of language depends on the cultural context (McCormack 2011c).

Pro-Gay Language

While gay discourse was a powerful concept for understanding the prevalence of phrases like "don't be gay" and "that's so gay," it was less effective in explaining another use of homosexually themed language. In McCormack and Anderson's (2010b) article on rugby players, they found that many heterosexual male athletes used homosexually themed language as a form of social bonding. In greeting one another, the men would often say "hey gay boy" or "hey sister." This language was used between friends in a welcoming manner. McCormack and Anderson argued that this could continue to privilege heterosexuality because of the framework of homosexual stigma that once existed in rugby. As McCormack (2011c) later argued, McCormack and Anderson were falling back on the same assumption of context that they had accused others of doing in labeling "that's so gay" as homophobic: a position that was aided by the fact that there were no openly gay athletes to judge this use of language within their research. Still, McCormack and Anderson provided no evidence that this privileged heterosexuality, and they should therefore not have drawn the conclusions they did.

In his ethnographic research on sixteen- to eighteen-year-old students in high schools in the United Kingdom, McCormack (2012) also documented the use of this form of language between gay and straight students as a way of bonding with each other. While playing sport or just hanging out, gay and straight students consciously adapted what they considered to be antiquated notions of sexuality and gender displays in order to develop their friendships.

Relating Language to Cultural Shifts

When outlining a typology of homosexually themed language, McCormack (2011c) argued that the effects of language were dependent on the cultural context in which they were used. Explicating this, he argued that the four forms of language discussed earlier will occur at discrete if overlapping cultural moments—dependent on the level of homophobia. McCormack was careful to highlight that this taxonomy was not intended to be a rigid description of the ever-changing relationship between sport cultures and language but rather to serve as a model that enabled people to correctly interpret different types of language.

First, in a highly homophobic culture, men use homophobic language to consolidate their own heterosexual identity and masculine standing (Plummer 1999). In this sport culture, homosexually themed language is indeed homophobic, as it is used with pernicious intent and has negative social effects, such as inhibiting gay athletes from coming out.

Second, in settings that are slightly less homophobic, boys and men call each other "fag" and other pejoratives that are both sexualized and gendered. Here, it is likely that many gay people will have negative experiences in sport; but it is also likely that there will be people who use these pejoratives who also support gay rights. In this culture, some young men will insist that their language use is not intended to stigmatize homosexuality, while others will use such pejoratives with pernicious intent. However, such pejoratives will continue to have negative social effects, including the regulation and restriction of acceptable masculine behaviors, because the intent of language use is not always clear.

Third, gay discourse occurs in settings where young men are not particularly concerned about whether they are socially perceived as gay. In settings of low homophobia, men say phrases like "that's so gay" as expressions of dissatisfaction and frustration. Importantly, there is no intent to marginalize or wound people with the use of this language. And while this is not necessarily pro-gay, young men maintain that the word "gay" does not connote same-sex desire in this context.

Finally, in gay-friendly cultures, athletes are not part of a homohysteric culture, and while they might prefer to be thought heterosexual, they do not control their behaviors to live up to a heteromasculine ideal. Here, homosexually themed language is used in a way that has *positive* social effects (McCormack 2012). Sometimes pro-gay language is said without any specific intention, but it is also used as a bonding mechanism between athletes by demonstrating emotional intimacy or inclusion of openly gay athletes. The fun and fundamentally friendly way this language is used—that is, the ease that straight athletes have with gay peers—helps contribute to a gay-friendly environment.

Conclusion

This chapter has identified the social and historical contexts, structures, and discourses that have influenced how sexualities and masculinities are perceived, enacted, and negotiated by male athletes. Highlighting the increasingly positive attitudes of heterosexual athletes toward their gay teammates in recent years, we have shown that no longer can all male athletes be stereotyped as inherently homophobic. Since the early 2000s there has been a vast cultural shift toward the acceptance of homosexuality, and although this has taken longer to transfer to the sport culture than to almost every other institution, the current generation of adolescent male athletes are breaking down the barriers of inequality. We can see this through the ever-increasing number of gay athletes who are coming out of the closet (Anderson 2011b) and the overwhelming acceptance they receive upon doing so. This is complemented with discussions about the emancipation of sexuality from the traditional heteronormative script and an increase in the willingness of heterosexual athletes to engage in lesbian, gay, bisexual, and transgender (LGBT) politics (see Outsports.com for many examples).

There have also been massive changes in recent years in the way homophobic language is used and interpreted by male athletes—from the highly homophobic language used to keep gay athletes closeted during the 1980s and early 1990s, to the current use of homophobic language as a way for heterosexual and gay athletes to bond with each other today (McCormack and Anderson 2010b). These changes have resulted from not only a decrease in homophobia but also a decrease in heterosexual men's fears of being thought gay—something we described as homohysteria.

The decline in cultural homohysteria has also benefited heterosexual male athletes, as they have been culturally granted an increasing variety of gendered behaviors without fear of stigma. This has led to greater tactility and emotional disclosure between athletes who no longer fear retribution for telling a teammate, "I love you, man." In fact, recent research on straight, undergraduate men in the United Kingdom shows that 90 percent have kissed another man on the lips (Anderson, Adams, and Rivers 2010). In our own ongoing research, we have shown that the custom of straight men kissing each other has also already taken hold in Australia and is beginning to take hold in the United States as well.

Finally, although the realm of sport has traditionally been a bastion of homophobia in contemporary Western societies (Anderson 2005a), we have now reached a time when it is erroneous to categorically label all sport as homophobic institutions in which heterosexuality is compulsory and gay athletes are marginalized. There is reason for optimism as new generations bring increasingly progressive attitudes toward homosexuality into our sport cultures.

4

Transsexual and Intersex Athletes

Erin E. Buzuvis

In August 2009, South African runner Caster Semenya competed in the World Championships in Berlin and won the 800-meter
event. But rumors and speculation surrounding her sex called her victory into question. Was Semenya really a woman? She came seemingly out of nowhere to dominate the race, posting a personal best
time (beating her previous record by seven seconds) that suggested
remarkable improvement over the course of the season. Her muscular
body and deep voice were also cause for suspicion. To find out for
sure, the international governing body for track and field, the International Amateur Athletics Federation (IAAF), requested that Semenya
submit to a medically supervised sex verification procedure. This request set off the most recent public controversy about sex and gender
in women's sport and raised challenging question about how
"woman" is defined.

Semenya is not the first athlete to have her eligibility for
women's sport called into question, and she probably won't be the
last. As long as the sporting world divides competitors into two dis-
tinct categories, male and female, there will be inquiries and assumptions about who belongs in which. What makes this categorization
difficult is that while the realm of sport divides the universe neatly
into male and female categories, nature does not. In Semenya's case,
the results of her sex verification test, which were thoughtlessly
leaked to the media, suggest that she has an intersex condition that
produces higher levels of the male hormone testosterone (perhaps

three times higher) than those of the average woman. This doesn't mean Semenya is a man. But it does mean that she does not have the typical physiology of most women. Does that mean she shouldn't compete as one?

The gender binary (the belief that everyone can be classified as either male or female by a set of deterministic and fixed criteria) presents challenges not only for athletes like Semenya who have intersex conditions but also for athletes who are transsexual. In 1977, for instance, Renee Richards famously challenged the US Tennis Association's (USTA) requirement that athletes must possess a pair of X chromosomes (the typical female karyotype) in order to qualify for the women's draw at the US Open. The USTA had devised this requirement in order to exclude Richards, who was born male (or rather, assigned a male sex at birth) and used surgery and hormones to physically transition to a female body, one that matched her female gender identity.

Unlike intersex conditions, which are, generally speaking, incongruities among the physical characteristics of sex, transsexuality is an incongruity between one's physical sex and one's gender identity. But like those with intersex conditions, transsexual athletes challenge the gender binary. Renee Richards, who identifies as female and who has a post-operative female body, is surely not a man. But the fact that she grew up in a male body makes her atypical of most women. Thus, Semenya, who has an intersex condition, and Richards, who is transsexual, both challenge the gender binary as atypical women. As this chapter explains, scrutiny and exclusion from women's sport stigmatizes intersex and transsexual athletes, but also female athletes at large, by constructing and reinforcing assumptions about female athletic difference and inferiority.

Gender 101: Defining Terms and Concepts

Before exploring the complexity of these issues, we must define the important foundational terminology and concepts. A good understanding of terms and concepts is a necessary first step toward understanding and ultimately dismantling sexual stigma in sport.

Sex vs. Gender

In everyday language, we often use the words *sex* and *gender* interchangeably. But in some contexts, like advocacy, research, and academia, these words are distinctly different. Sex refers to the biological or physiological attributes that make someone male or female. When a baby is born, a doctor may declare, "It's a boy" after scrutinizing the physical evidence that is the baby's genitalia. The doctor is assuming that if the baby has male genitalia, he also has a male (XY) chromosome pattern, internal genitalia that will produce male hormones (androgens, and specifically testosterone), and that these hormones will cause the body to produce physical characteristics that are typical of the male sex. A similar, opposite set of assumptions is made when the doctor declares, "It's a girl." These assumptions tend to be true in most cases.

But this information about an individual's sex does not necessarily tell us anything about his or her gender. Gender refers to an individual's identification *with* and expression *of* his or her sex. It is often said that gender is to sex as femininity is to female (or as masculinity is to male). Gender is informed by the biology of sex, but is specifically an expression and identity of that sex that is filtered through the individual's psychology and social environment.

Intersexuals

"Intersex" is an umbrella term used to describe various conditions in which the physical attributes of sex are incongruous, not entirely male or entirely female. Sometimes these incongruities are produced at the chromosomal level, such as when an individual's sex chromosomes defy the typically XX (female) or XY (male) pattern. Individuals with intersex conditions may instead have such patterns as XO, XXY, XYY, or XXX. The result of such chromosomal patterns may produce atypical physical characteristics ranging from extra height (such as in the case of XYY males) to reduced fertility, ambiguous genitalia, and androgyny. But not every individual with a chromosomal anomaly will express this condition, and many will not even know that they have it unless they are tested for some reason. This high degree of variability in the expression of such conditions is due in part to a sometimes coexisting condition called mosaicism, in which only some of the body's cells have the atypical sex chromosome patterns, while other cells are either all XX or all XY.

Other intersex conditions affect hormones rather than chromosomes. For example, androgen insensitivity syndrome occurs in individuals who have a male (XY) chromosomal pattern, which triggers the production of male hormones called androgens. But due to this syndrome, the body lacks or has diminished capacity to respond to these masculinizing hormones, so the body will develop entirely or at least partially in a female manner. Another such condition is congenital adrenal hyperplasia, which causes individuals with XX chromosomes to have masculine genitalia. Other conditions that affect physical development in utero or at puberty produce internal and external genitalia that defy classification as entirely male or female; indeed, for 1 out of every 1,500 to 2,000 births, an expert in sex differentiation must be called in to interpret atypical presentation of the baby's gender (Fausto-Sterling 2000).

Due to this wide variety of intersex conditions, it is neither possible nor appropriate to make generalizations about how individuals with an intersex condition experience their condition, the physical effects of an intersex condition, or how and whether such a condition affects their gender identity. For some whose intersex condition is invisible, either because it could only be detected by medical testing or because of surgical intervention at birth, they might have a gender identity that is unaffected by their condition. For example, several female athletes in history, Semenya being the latest example, learned of their intersex condition when they were forced to participate in gender testing as a condition for participating in the Olympics or other world-class athletic events. Prior to that time, they never questioned their femaleness, because in every physical and psychological way that mattered, these athletes were female.

Transgender Individuals and Transsexuals

Though usage may vary by context, "transgender" is commonly defined as an umbrella term that may be claimed by anyone whose gender identity does not match the sex they were assigned at birth. The transgender label may include those who are "transsexual," meaning they identify with the gender that is opposite from which they were assigned, as well as those whose gender identity does not fall into either category represented by the gender binary (Feinberg 1996). "Gender queer," "bigender," and "androgyne" are examples of some of the ways transgender individuals in this latter category may describe their gender identity. Because one's gender identity may not be obvious, it is usually more respectful to ask which pronoun a person prefers rather than to presume based on the person's appearance.

Transsexual individuals may or may not undergo hormone treatment, surgery, or both to conform to the sex with which they identify. A male-to-female transsexual—that is, a person assigned a male sex at birth but who identifies as female—may take androgen blockers to negate the affects of testosterone, as well as estrogen to promote the growth of breast tissue and other aspects of a female-shaped body. She also may elect surgeries to remove her penis and testes or to augment her breasts (W-PATH 2001). A female-to-male transsexual may take testosterone to masculinize his body, and may elect for surgery to remove his breasts. Surgeries to construct a penis (called phalloplasty) are also available, though less frequently preformed. Some transsexual individuals do not undergo either hormonal or surgical modification for reasons including expense (as treatments are often excluded from insurance coverage) and personal preference. Within the transsexual community, the labels "pre-operative, "post-operative," and "non-operative" (or "pre-op," "post-op," and "non-op" for short) distinguish between transsexuals who are awaiting surgery, who have had surgery, and who are not planning to have surgery.

Intersex and Transsexual Athletes in History

Intersex Athletes

The first known intersex Olympic athlete was Stella Walsh, who won a silver medal in the women's 100-meter sprint in 1936, and who was posthumously discovered to have ambiguous genitalia and chromosomes after an autopsy was performed on her body in 1980 (Ritchie, Reynard, and Lewis 2008). The International Olympic Committee (IOC) began requiring women to submit to mandatory sex verification testing during the Cold War, which raised the geopolitical stakes of the Olympic medal count. Many presumed that sport ministries in Eastern European countries were engaging in gender fraud to dominate women's sport in the service of nationalist objectives.

In 1968 the IOC replaced the visual inspection method of sex verification testing (commonly called "nude parades") with a chromosome test to determine athletes' eligibility for women's sports. Specifically, this test counted whether an athlete had a second X chromosome, on the belief that this would allow sport organizers to distinguish women (typically XX) from men (typically XY). Not surprisingly, such testing did not accurately sort competitors with intersex conditions that produce various chromosome patterns including XXY (an individual who would have passed the test, despite appearing male by virtue of the Y chromosome) or single-X (also written

XO) (an individual who is not male, but would have failed the test for lacking a second X). Polish sprinter Eva Klobukowska was the first athlete banned from women's sport and stripped of her Olympic medals after genetic testing revealed anomalous sex chromosomes in some cells (likely an XX/XY mosaicism) (Wackwitz 2003). Twenty years later, another high-profile runner, Maria Jose Martinez Patino, discovered for the first time during a sex verification test that she had male XY chromosomes, and was later diagnosed with androgen insensitivity syndrome, discussed previously (Wackwitz 2003). She was reinstated by the IAAF after she proved that the syndrome rendered her body incapable of responding to the testosterone that her body produced in response to the presence of a Y chromosome (Ritchie, Reynard, and Lewis 2008).

Eventually the IOC switched to a different method of chromosome testing that disqualified athletes from women's sport based on the presence of a Y chromosome rather than the absence of a second X. Yet even this method of testing produced many false positives, such as in 1996 when 8 of the over 3,000 female athletes tested for the Atlanta Summer Olympic Games tested positive for a Y chromosome but were permitted to compete after further testing revealed that these athletes were insensitive to testosterone. Significantly, chromosome testing never revealed a single case of gender fraud—male athletes pretending to be women. Many criticized the practice for excluding or causing stress and anxiety among athletes with intersex conditions for whom no biological basis existed for exclusion from women's sport, as well as for affronting the dignity and privacy of all female athletes who were forced to submit to testing.

In response to such criticism, the IOC abandoned compulsory sex verification testing for women's events in 1999, but it and the IAAF allow testing on a case-by-case basis in response to suspicion of gender fraud. Suspicion-based testing revealed the intersex condition of Indian runner Santhi Soundarajan, who was stripped of her silver medal in the 2006 Asia Games, and most recently South African sprinter Caster Semenya after her victory in the 800 meters at the 2009 World Championships. The IAAF's decision to sex-test Semenya subjected the eighteen-year-old to public criticism and scrutiny into intimate and personal matters. The IAAF has ruled that she may keep her medal from the 2009 World Championships, and recently cleared her to compete in future women's events.

Transsexual Athletes

In 1977, American tennis player Renee Richards, a male-to-female transsexual, competed in the US Women's Open after winning a lawsuit against the US Tennis Association, which had tried to exclude Richards on the basis of her XY chromosomes. A New York State court rejected the USTA's argument that male-to-female transsexual athletes have a competitive advantage when competing against other women. Medical experts and fellow tennis player Billie Jean King testified for Richards, supporting Richards's claim that estrogen treatments and surgical removal of her testes made her a woman "for all intents and purposes" with no discernable competitive advantage. The court also rejected the USTA's claim that a chromosome test was necessary to prevent female imposters from trying to enter women's sporting events, dismissing the organization's claim that a male who is not transsexual would elect to go through surgery and hormones to feminize his body just to compete in women's sport. The court's decision that the USTA discriminated against Richards in violation of state antidiscrimination law paved the way for Richards to compete in the 1977 US Open, where she lost in the semifinal round.

In addition to Richards's historic example, male-to-female transsexual athletes compete in contemporary women's sports as well. Two examples come from the sport of golf. In 2004, Danish-born, Australian-based golfer Mianne Bagger became the first transsexual woman to compete in a professional golf tournament, having surgically transitioned from male to female in 1995. Another transsexual golfer, Lana Lawless, won the Women's World Long Drive Championship in 2008. Michelle Dumaresq, a Canadian mountain bike racer, has competed in women's events since 2001, six years after her surgical transition from male to female. Even more recently, Canadian short-track cyclist Kristen Worley nearly qualified for the 2008 Beijing Olympics after transitioning from male to female.

In contrast to the examples of male-to-female transsexual athletes, there are fewer well-known athletes who have transitioned from female to male. Alyn Libman competed as a male on the University of California–Berkeley club figure-skating team and under the auspices of US Figure Skating. Libman's transition from female to male began while in high school and included a physical transition induced by testosterone. Other female-to-male transsexuals elect to forgo or delay a physical transition in order to remain eligible for women's sports. Keelin Godsey, an All-American hammer thrower, identified and expressed as male when he competed on the Bates College women's track and field team in 2005, and he continues to do so today as he trains as an Olympic hopeful in the women's hammer throw. Similarly, Kye Allums continued to play women's basketball for George Washington University, even after coming out about his male gender identity. Like Godsey, Allums decided to forgo a physical transition during college in order to remain eligible for women's sport.

Current Policies Governing Intersex and Transgender Athletes

Sex Verification Policies and Intersex Athletes

In 1996 the International Olympic Committee stopped requiring all female athletes to submit to compulsory sex verification testing as a condition for participation in women's sport. This change was prompted by concern for the dignity and privacy of female athletes, diminished concern about men fraudulently competing as women (a rare to nonexistent occurrence), and a recognition that gender is more complex than a chromosome test can reveal (Simpson, Ljungqvist, and Ferguson-Smith 2000).

Though no governing body of sport continues to use chromosome testing to identify and exclude athletes with intersex conditions, many allow some manner of sex verification testing on a case-by-case basis. Rather than a chromosome test, an athlete whose female sex is under suspicion must submit to an examination conducted by a panel of medical and psychological experts for a holistic evaluation. It was just such a panel that examined Caster Semenya and produced conclusions that her elevated levels of testosterone did not disqualify her from women's sport. Based on these conclusions, the IAAF cleared Semenya to continue to compete in women's events.

Subsequently, in 2011, the IOC and other international sport federations adopted a policy to provide clearer standards in future cases involving female athletes who have elevated levels of male hormones (androgens), including testosterone. Women typically have serum testosterone levels around one nanomoles per liter (Devries 2008), but some women may have elevated testosterone levels due to normal variation, athletic training, or endocrine disorders that may or may not be related to an intersex condition. According to this new policy, a woman whose blood reveals elevated levels of testosterone will be allowed to participate in women's sports as long as her levels are below the normal male range of ten nanomoles per liter, or she has androgen resistance (such as androgen insensitivity syndrome) and thus "derives no competitive advantage from having androgen levels in the normal male range" (IAAF 2011).

While its supporters tout the policy as necessary to provide fairness and clarity regarding questions about eligibility for women's sports, others have criticized and questioned it. Some, like Yale endocrinologist Myron Genel, who consults with the IOC on gender policies, have questioned whether sport should be singling out naturally occurring hormones as the only source of competitive advantage in order to warrant exclusion from sport (Marchant 2011). Women with naturally high testosterone are similar to women who are naturally tall or naturally strong in that all may be naturally more inclined toward success in sport (Dreger 2010). Yet the realm of sport doesn't exclude women whose height or weight or musculature is "in the normal male range." Other critics have questioned why concerns about testosterone fairness are raised only in women's sports.

Male athletes aren't tested and excluded for having natural testosterone levels above or below the "normal male range," and this double standard promotes the view that female athletes are in need of this special protection while male athletes are not. Finally, the fact that testing of female athletes occurs in response to suspicion about their masculinity means it can be deployed to target any female athlete whose appearance or performance fails to conform to stereotyped notions of femininity. Because these stereotypes are most often generated by reference to the dominant white culture, suspicion-based testing has the potential to disproportionately affect female athletes of color like Semenya (Smith 2009). Sex verification testing of any kind also endorses the cultural tendency to question the femininity of any woman who demonstrates too much of the very attributes that are prized in sport, like strength and speed.

Transsexual Athlete Policies

The IOC was also on the forefront of policy formation regarding transsexual athletes' participation in Olympic and international elite sport. In 2004 the IOC became the first sport organization to promulgate a policy designed to allow participation by transsexual athletes consistent with their transitioned sex. In order to qualify, an athlete must meet the following criteria:

- Surgical anatomical changes have been completed, including external genitalia changes and gonadectomy;
- Legal recognition of their assigned sex has been conferred by the appropriate official authorities; and
- Hormonal therapy appropriate for the assigned sex has been administered in a verifiable manner and for a sufficient length of time to minimize gender-related advantages in sport competitions [later defined as a minimum of two years from the time of surgery]. (IOC 2003)

Many other sport organizations have adopted the IOC's policy as their own, including USA Track and Field, USA Rugby, USA Hockey, the US Golf Association, the Ladies Professional Golf Association, the Ladies Golf Union (Great Britain), the Ladies European Golf Tour, Women's Golf Australia, USA Track and Field, and the Gay and Lesbian International Sports Association, as well as at least one association—the Connecticut Interscholastic Athletic Association—that administers sport at the high school level (Buzuvis 2011).

Yet notwithstanding this widespread adoption, the IOC's policy is also not without critics. While the policy upends the outdated default presumption that only one's sex at birth is relevant to determining one's eligibility for sport, several aspects of the policy render it vulnerable to charges of being unnecessarily restrictive. The requirement that a transsexual athlete change his or her legal documentation to reflect the new sex, for example, has no bearing on one's athletic ability. Moreover, some countries and states have laws that make it comparatively harder (if not impossible) to change one's sex, so this requirement would have the effect of excluding some athletes for reasons having nothing to do with sport. There is also no medical reason to require surgical transformation for either transsexual women (who do not require a gonadectomy to reduce testosterone levels if they are taking androgen blockers as required by the hormone criterion) or transsexual men (for whom the surgical reconstruction of a penis is prohibitively expensive and not even plausibly related to athletic performance) (Griffin and Carroll 2010). A requirement of sex reassignment surgery to participate in youth sport, such as contemplated by the high school sport policy in Connecticut, operates as an effective ban on all participation by transsexual athletes, given that sex reassignment surgery is not medically recommended for individuals under eighteen years of age except in rare cases (W-PATH 2001). Even the requirement to spend two years on hormones has been criticized as overly restrictive, as medical evidence increasingly suggests that hormone treatments take full affect after one year (Devries 2008).

For these reasons, advocates are urging college and high school athletic associations in the United States not to adopt the IOC policy as their own. The first organization to break with the IOC's approach was the Washington Interscholastic Athletic Association (WIAA), which decided in 2007 to allow high school and middle school athletes to compete "in a manner that is consistent with their gender identity, irrespective of the gender listed on a student's records" (WIAA 2010:para. 18.15.0). The WIAA's policy includes a procedure for handling questions as to whether a student's request to participate consistent with their gender identity is "bona fide," but does not require any medical evidence to support the student's right to play. Rather, the policy allows the student to attest for him- or herself that his or her gender identity is consistent, or a parent or healthcare provider may do so on the student's behalf. This policy has been praised by advocates who argue that high school and middle school sports should be as inclusive as possible (Griffin and Carroll 2010) and that other states, most of which have not adopted any kind of transgender inclusion policy, use the WIAA's as a model.

At the college level, the National Collegiate Athletic Association created a policy governing participation of transsexual athletes (NCAA 2011). The NCAA's policy does not impose any surgical or legal requirements on athletes wishing to play in accordance with their identified sex rather than their birth sex. It expressly allows female-to-male transsexual athletes who are not transitioning with hormones to continue to be eligible for women's sports. Those who do wish to transition with hormones are eligible for men's sports after receiving a medical exemption from the ban on exogenous testosterone. The NCAA's policy also allows athletes transitioning from male to female to compete in women's sports after they have undergone hormone treatment for one year, as long as they continue that treatment throughout their playing career.

This policy is consistent with recommendations contained in a report called "On the Team," issued in the fall of 2010 by two prominent advocacy groups, the National Center for Lesbian Rights and the Women's Sports Foundation (Griffin and Carroll 2010). It replaces the NCAA's earlier, nonbinding guidance document that had suggested schools classify athletes according to their legal identification, such as the sex designation on a birth certificate, passport, or driver's license (McKindra 2006), a position that did not resolve questions of a transsexual athlete's eligibility in a fair or consistent manner because the requirements for changing one's legal identification differed by state.

The Stigmatizing Potential of Transgender and Intersex Athlete Policies

Transgender athletes and those with intersex conditions who participate in accordance with their identified sex are often criticized by those who believe, however erroneously, that they are fraudulent competitors or that they compete at an advantage relative to the rest of the field. For example, opponents of Canadian mountain bike racer Michelle Dumaresq challenged the national governing body's determination of her eligibility for women's events, even though Dumaresq had transitioned surgically, hormonally, and legally. After the failed attempts of Dumaresq's opponents to disqualify her by petition and appeal, one competitor, a runner-up to Dumaresq's first-place finish, resorted to protest by joining her on the medal podium with a t-shirt that read: "100% Pure Woman Champ" (Morris 2006). In a more recent example, the press reported on the quiet grumbling of Caster Semenya's competitors upon her reinstatement to women's track (Hart 2010).

At the same time, there is also evidence of increasing acceptance for transgender athletes. Keelin Godsey and Kye Allums, two former college athletes who participated in women's sports while identifying as male, both received support and acceptance from their coaches and teammates (Brady 2010b; Torre and Epstein 2012; Woog 2011). For Allums's team, the media's scrutiny of his public transgender identity was a larger obstacle to team unity than the fact of that identity itself (Torre and Epstein 2012). There is evidence of emerging acceptance within individual sports as well, as female golfers have publicly endorsed male-to-female transsexual golfers Lana Lawless's and Mianne Bagger's participation in women's events (Calkins 2008; Passa 2005). Mountain bike racer Missy Giove advocated for the inclusion of her competitor Dumaresq as well (Billman 2004). Judging by these examples, athletes are not of one mind when it comes to participation by intersex and transgender athletes. Yet the examples of athlete support for transgender and intersex competitors and teammates suggest that policies of inclusion have the potential to promote the kind of contact among athletes that reduces the stereotypes and misinformation that lead to bias. When athletes speak publicly about their views, they have the potential to influence society as well.

But just as policies of inclusion have the potential to reduce stereotypes and bias against intersex and transgender athletes, they also have the potential to promote stigma, and in a variety of ways. First and foremost, any policy that allows athletes to participate only in accordance with their assigned sex at birth ignores the significance of gender identity and the role that it must play in making appropriate classifications. For example, when the USTA attempted to exclude Renee Richards from women's competition in the US Open because of her male chromosomes, it was ignoring or minimizing her self-identification as a woman. The USTA's policy in that case stigmatized Richards by suggesting to her and to the wider sporting world that she was not a real woman, that her female gender identity was not genuine or deeply felt. When supporters of the USTA's policy suggested that allowing Richards to play could lead other men to physically transition just to be able compete in women's tennis, they put Richards in the same category as other, fictional, masqueraders whose gender identities were not genuine. By extension, the suggestion was that Richards herself was also a fraud. In reality, gender identity is not something that individuals casually decide. It is not like choosing a political party or even a religion; it is something a person experiences rather than selects. Most of us are not conscious of experiencing a gender identity, because our gender identities are not contested. But individuals whose gender identity is different from the sex they are assigned at birth are likely to be highly conscious of their gender identity and prioritize it as a factor in their self-determination. Consequently, it ought to be respected and considered to the fullest possible extent whenever sex-based classifications are being made.

Fortunately, awareness of the significance of gender identity in determining an athlete's sex classification is growing in sport. The IOC's transgender athlete policy, for all the criticism described previously, was a huge step in this direction because it abandoned the prior assumption that gender identity didn't matter—if you were born into a male body, there was no chance of competing in women's sport no matter how you identified and how your body might have

been surgically or hormonally altered. Similarly, its hyperandrogenism policy is also a step toward fairness for intersex athletes, who
have historically risked exclusion from women's sport under policies
that determined eligibility based only on chromosomes.

Yet policies like the IOC's, which have been implemented to promote inclusion of intersex and transgender athletes, have the potential to promote stigma. One way is by excluding more athletes than
any measure of fairness requires, such as by including requirements
for surgical and legal sex change, which are not linked to sport performance, or by requiring a two-year period of hormone treatment
when one year is what seems to suffice. By overregulating participation of transgender athletes in these ways, sport organizations send
the message that the excluded athletes matter less than the practical,
political benefits of conforming a policy to baseless assumptions and
stereotypes about sex and gender.

Transgender and intersex athlete participation policies are also
potentially stigmatizing when they reflect unwarranted, disproportionate, or one-sided concerns about competitive equity. In this context, competitive equity is the belief that some individuals must be
excluded from (women's) sport in order to preserve the fairness of
the game or event. This belief is rooted in the assumption that
women are categorically inferior as athletes compared to men. Only
that assumption would explain why men (or those who appear too
much like men) are *necessarily* assumed to have a competitive advantage just because they are men, regardless of other factors that
also affect performance.

This is a hard assumption to question. After all, anyone can see
that there are generalized differences between male and female bodies, owing to the tendency for men to have higher levels of testosterone, which contributes to bone and muscle strength (Devries
2008). Anyone who has observed sport knows that, compared to
women, men usually run faster, dunk higher, and hit harder. But this
doesn't mean, when it comes to sex and sport, that biology is destiny.
We've all seen exceptions to the rule. Consider the most recent
Boston Marathon. The first-place woman was slower than the first-
place man by almost twenty minutes, but she finished in 31st overall—which means she beat 13,809 of the 13,839 men who finished
the race. If biological sex were solely or primarily determinative of
athletic success, we would expect her to have finished 13,840th. To
further refute the suggestion that one's sexual biology is determinative of athletic talent, there is also increasing evidence that access to

opportunity, which women have only recently begun to gain in any manner or scope approaching men's access, is leveling the field. In running, for example, the difference between men's and women's records has actually been closing in recent decades, and women's records have eclipsed men's in some of the longest-distance races, like ultra-marathons (Cavanagh and Sykes 2006). Relatedly, studies showing that girls and boys can learn to throw equally well with their nondominant (i.e., untrained) arm suggest that many athletic skills are learned rather than biologically determined (Dowling 2000; Williams, Haywood, and Painter 1996).

This doesn't mean that sex classifications in sport are obsolete and unnecessary. Women have not had equal access to sporting opportunities for long enough (if at all) to close the performance gap in most sports, so women's sports play an important role in preserving opportunities for women that would otherwise be lost if opportunities were distributed only based on athletic skill and talent (Dreger 2010). But this doesn't mean that the fairness of the game or event necessarily requires sport to strictly control sex classifications, especially at the margins of those classifications where transgender and intersex athletes may find themselves. The world of sport, including women's sport, is already highly tolerant of a wide variety of potential sources of competitive advantage (Reeser 2005). Excluding a transgender or intersex athlete based on concerns that he or she might be, for example, taller than the average girl makes little sense when sport does not already exclude *girls* who are taller than the average girl. The reason why we don't worry too much about the competitive advantage of taller girls over shorter girls also applies to transgender and intersex athletes: many other factors contribute to athletic talent and success. No one would play basketball, for instance, if it were a forgone conclusion that the team with the tallest player wins. Instead, we know that training, intelligence, mental attitude, coaching, health, and even luck contribute as much to a player's or a team's performance as any physical characteristic that might generally differ between the sexes. As medical experts have said, even any potential advantages one might have by virtue of being intersex or transgender are "no different from other naturally occurring physical advantages like being taller or having more balance" (Handley 2010).

The IOC's policies for transgender and intersex athletes single out sex-related characteristics as the only naturally occurring source of (presumed) competitive advantage as a basis for exclusion, and as such, they risk promoting the assumption that all female athletes are categorically inferior. This belief is underscored by the one-sidedness of such policies: competitive equity must be strictly regulated in women's sport. A woman with high testosterone levels may be excluded under the IOC's hyperandrogenism policy, but in men's sport, a higher-than-average level of naturally occurring testosterone is considered just another natural source of competitive advantage (Crincoli 2011). This double standard reflects and contributes to society's uneasiness with women who do not conform to society's expectations that women should be athletically inferior, a stereotype that challenges the legitimacy of all female athletes (Cavanagh and Sykes 2006). Both the IOC's hyperandrogenism policy, as well its transgender athlete policy, redefine the category of "woman" in a way that reinforces a normal definition of female (not transgender, not intersex, not masculine) against which all women will be measured, possibly scrutinized, and in some cases excluded.

Such policies also stigmatize individual athletes who may be excluded by reason of their transsexual or intersex identity because they send the message that the right of these individuals to participate is not worth the effort it would take to overturn some unwarranted assumptions. When these policies are replicated at the high school level, as the IOC's transgender athletic policy has been in Connecticut, the stigmatizing potential is magnified. In the educational context, there are many reasons to extend participation opportunities to transgender and intersex athletes that relate to the educational mission of high school and college sports, which extends to helping students develop interpersonal skills, self-esteem, and character. Excluding transgender and intersex athletes, who might have even more to gain from sport participation given the social challenges of being different, sends a disheartening message to them that the school does not support their educational development or their right to equal opportunity (Buzuvis 2011).

In contrast to the IOC's policies, a policy that allows athletes to compete as female as long as they consistently and genuinely identify as female, such as the Washington Interscholastic Athletic Association's policy, has less stigmatizing potential. It does not overregulate eligibility or reflect unnecessary or disproportionate concerns about competitive equity. It avoids inferiorizing girls and women's sports by refraining from the suggestion that girls in general are threatened by some girls who are different. Yet even a policy like the WIAA's has a stigmatizing potential not yet discussed. While such a policy honors the rights of students to define themselves as the sex other than their assigned sex, it does nothing for transgender students whose gender identities are neither male nor female: Which sports should they play? Such an omission could contribute to the erasure of transgender identities that are not transsexual.

One possible way to minimize this potential erasure and promote inclusion of gender identities that are more complicated than our binary paradigm allows is to integrate girls' and boys' sports. In coed sports, no one is excluded by virtue of their sex or gender. As noted previously, there are good reasons to separate sports by sex—preserving opportunities for women and girls and accounting for what are real, if not necessarily fixed, differences in skills and talents. But this doesn't mean all sports must be separate. Affording all students greater access to coed opportunities would promote inclusion of transgender athletes and, likely as well, many nontransgender athletes who might feel more comfortable in an integrated environment that allows for a greater range of gender identities to be expressed. Coed sports can also help mitigate the stigma that women's sports are categorically inferior to men's, a stigma that is promoted by the strict, pervasive, and widespread separation of sport by sex (McDonagh and Pappano 2008).

Conclusion

By recognizing the right of athletes to self-define based on their gender identity in at least some cases, policies affecting transgender and intersex athletes' eligibility for sport are reducing the stigma caused by exclusion. However, the limits that remain should still be examined as remaining sources of stigma. Policies that allow athletes to define themselves based on their gender identity, as well as policies that add coed options to the menu of sporting opportunities, have the greatest potential to reduce the stigmatization of affected athletes, as well as of women and girls as a whole.

5

Taking Account of Race

Nefertiti A. Walker

In 2005, Sheryl Swoopes, of the Women's National Basketball Association (WNBA), became the most distinguished and successful athlete, male or female, to come out as having a same-sex partner (Granderson 2005). In her interview with *ESPN Magazine,* she claimed that she had not come out to become a hero for the gay community or gay supporters and allies. Rather, Swoopes had come out to rid herself of the stress she experienced in hiding who she really was, an African American lesbian. As Swoopes stated during the interview: "I'm just at a point in my life where I'm tired of having to pretend to be somebody I'm not. I'm tired of having to hide my feelings about the person I care about. About the person I love" (Granderson 2005:1). Swoopes's accolades included a National Collegiate Athletic Association (NCAA) Division I national championship victory, an NCAA Division I national player-of-the-year award, three Olympic gold medals, four WNBA championship victories, and three regular-season WNBA most-valuable-player awards. Yet she called life in the closet "miserable" (Granderson 2005). Swoopes's coming out was met with either welcoming comments or insistence that her sexuality was completely irrelevant. The lesbian, gay, bisexual, and transgender (LGBT) community met Swoopes with open arms and was thankful to have such a strong representative (Buzinski 2005). The online commentary on lesbian blogs and discussion boards was also positive. At that point in her career, Swoopes was being endorsed by Nike and had even had a Nike shoe named after her, the Air Swoopes. Many would have presumed that, overall, Swoopes's coming out was a success.

In 2011, six years after being the first African American woman in sport to come out as having a same-sex partner, Sheryl Swoopes announced that she was engaged to a man. This may have come as a shock to many, especially considering the media frenzy surrounding her coming out in 2005. Viewing sexuality as a binary of two categories (homosexual and heterosexual), as opposed to a fluid continuum, much of society was confused by Swoopes's announcement of being engaged to a man. Mainstream media stood clear of the discussion altogether. Many LGBT bloggers and members of online community websites expressed mixed feelings. Some took this opportunity to explain the continuum that is sexuality, while others condemned her seemingly indecisive bisexual behavior.

Meanwhile, the black online community, who during her 2005 announcement of being in a same-sex relationship had remained rather quiet, also expressed mixed feelings. Online blogs such as *Black Love and Marriage* were filled with posts expressing support for Swoopes, with bloggers commending her move in the "right" direction or insisting that they had always known she would turn her life around sooner or later. Other blogs such as *Black Media Scoop* seemed more supportive of her happiness and less concerned with her sexuality. Whereas the LGBT community felt partially abandoned by the fact Sheryl Swoopes was engaging in a heterosexual relationship, the African American community seemed to be uncertain of their feelings about her choice. As discussed in this chapter, while African Americans tend to express less favorable attitudes toward such same-sex issues as marriage, they also are less likely to openly take a stance against individuals' civil rights and employment rights for LGBT individuals (Lewis 2003). Therefore, the fact that blacks did not publicly speak out against this black LGBT athlete should not be surprising.

As another example, Kye Allums is an African American, transgender man who was born female. Allums played on the women's basketball team at George Washington University. Allums decided, before his junior season, to publicly come out as a transgender man. In a statement to the Associated Press, Allums talked about the support he had received from the university during his transition. "This means a lot," he said. "I didn't choose to be born in this body and feel the way I do. I decided to transition—that is, change my name and pronouns—because it bothered me to hide who I am, and I am trying to help myself and others be who they are" (Associated Press 2010).

Allums wanted to continue to play for the women's basketball team and said he would not begin any form of hormonal treatment, and therefore remain biologically female, just as he had been since birth. However, Allums wanted to change his name from Kyler Kelcian Allums, his birth name, to Kye Allums. Allums also asked to be referred to with male pronouns. In an interview with *USA Today,* Allums explained his identity frankly: "Yes, I am a male on a female team. And I want to be clear about this. I am a transgender male, which means feelings-wise, how it feels on the inside, I feel as if I should have been born male with male parts. But my biological sex is female, which makes me a transgender male" (Brady 2010b:1).

The overall attitude of the online commentary regarding Allums's coming out was very supportive. All of the three media sources that I analyzed (CNN.com, ESPN.com, and USAToday.com) were objective and stuck to the facts (seemingly to avoid offending anyone); if any opinions were expressed, they were in support of Allums.

Race and Sexuality

This chapter discusses and analyzes the dynamic relationship between race and sexual orientation in sport. In recent years, there has been an increase in awareness of sexual minorities and the role they play in society commensurate with increased visibility of groups such as the Human Rights Campaign and even more specialized organizations such as the National Center for Lesbian Rights. These organizations, along with a host of others, work to provide a safe space and equal rights for sexual minorities. Arguably one of the most visible recent wins for groups that fight for the rights of sexual minorities was the 2011 repeal of the US military's "don't ask, don't tell" policy. This policy, which had been in place since 1993, allowed closeted gays and lesbians to serve in the military, while strictly prohibiting openly gay and lesbian individuals from serving (Miles 2011). Although there have been such efforts to make American culture more welcoming to and inclusive of sexual minorities, the sport world remains a hostile environment for sexual minorities (Anderson 2005a; Griffin 1998; Iannotta and Kane 2002).

Many would argue that American culture has made considerable strides toward becoming more inclusive. In 2008, the American people voted into office their first president of color. Although Barack Obama is of mixed race (his mother is a white American and his father is Kenyan), he was born in the United States and is routinely categorized by the media as African American. This in itself is a tremendous step toward acceptance of people of color in leadership positions. Recall that it was not until 1964 that the civil rights of people of color became legally protected. Thus the election of a president who partially identifies as African American provides evidence of a society ready to move forward from a past founded on discrimination and the withholding of civil liberties and rights based on gender, race, and ethnicity. Although the American people seem optimistic about their progress as a nation based on equality, the world of sport continues to reignite remnants of the nineteenth and twentieth centuries, with inequality based on race and sexuality still acting as a barrier to the advancement of these minority groups (Greene 2000).

Similar to race, the topic of sexuality seems to be progressing away from its taboo role in American culture. It is now legal for same-sex couples to marry in a handful of US states. Similarly, same-sex relationships are now playing intricate roles on primetime American television. Most recently, *Modern Family,* a 2010 winner of the primetime Emmy for best comedy, showcases a multicultural and sexually diverse family in which two of the main characters are gay men and are in a monogamous relationship with each other. The presence of *Modern Family,* as well as recent gay and lesbian–themed movies such as the 2010 American film *The Kids Are All Right,* gives support to the contention that American society, specifically the entertainment industry, is becoming more welcoming to and accepting of same-sex lifestyles. Likewise in the music industry, Lady Gaga, who according to *Forbes* was the most influential celebrity in the world in 2011, recently dressed as a man for the MTV Music Awards. Lady Gaga routinely advocates for equality regardless of sexual preference and race/ethnicity, and even supported the campaign against the US military's "don't ask, don't tell" policy.

Despite these examples, sexual diversity is not widely accepted in the sport context. In fact, the world of sport might even serve as a fertile environment for perpetuating prejudicial practices against sexual minorities. How do racial prejudice and sexual prejudice intersect in the world of sport and result in the formation of multiple unique identities for those who are both racial and sexual minorities? Since there is very little sport research that examines sexual minorities who are not of African American or Caucasian descent, I focus here on black and white sexual minorities in American sport.

Racial Prejudice in Sport

Race in sport is a topic that has been discussed in depth in the sport literature. At the collegiate level, black coaches are routinely underrepresented, although black athletes make up a large percentage of the players on most NCAA teams. The same is true, but to a lesser extent, for blacks in professional sport. As evidenced by the two stories that open this chapter, basketball seems to boast some of the greatest racial diversity in sport (Lapchick 2010a, 2010b). In college basketball (NCAA Division I), blacks compose 60 percent of men's basketball players and 50 percent of women's basketball players (DeHass 2009). However, blacks (both male and female) compose 27 percent of the head coaches in men's college basketball and 21 of the head coaches in women's college basketball (Zgonc 2010). Thus in college basketball there is a discrepancy between the percentage of blacks who play and the percentage of blacks who lead. Similar inequalities can be seen in basketball at the professional level.

According to Richard Lapchick (2010a), for men, blacks compose 77 percent of all players in the National Basketball Association (NBA). However, blacks compose only 27 percent of the head coaches, 2 percent of the majority owners, and 21 percent of the other professional employees among the league. Likewise for women, in the WNBA, blacks compose 69 percent of all players, but only 33 percent of head coaches, none of the majority owners, and 24 percent of the other professional employees among the league. Again, we see that blacks compose the majority of the players, but are vastly underrepresented in leadership positions. Basketball is one of the most popular team sports for blacks, both women and men. Basketball is culturally accepted in the black community and is role-modeled as an acceptable sport to participate in from a very young age through adulthood. Nonetheless, the black presence among the leadership in basketball, at both the collegiate and professional levels, remains limited.

Researchers have long sought to understand why this phenomenon exists for blacks in sport. Why do blacks have access to certain sports as athletes, but not as coaches or in other roles of leadership? One such theory is that racism is institutionalized in sport (Cunningham 2010c; Eitzen and Sage 2003; Singer 2005). John Singer (2005) uses critical race theory (CRT) as an epistemology for exploring the experiences of black male athletes with racism in intercollegiate sport. This theory posits four main themes. First, CRT puts forth that racism is deeply ingrained in American culture such that racism is embedded in all social institutions (e.g., law, education, etc.). Second, CRT questions whether current civil rights laws are all-encompassing and believes that these laws failed to completely consider all the inequalities that African Americans endure. CRT also questions the validity of concepts such as meritocracy, objectivity, color blindness, and neutrality, and CRT believes that the experiential knowledge of people of color remains unacknowledged. Adopting this theoretical framework, Singer found that African American athletes feel they suffered differential treatment compared to their white counterparts, and that they were deprived of access to leadership positions in sport.

The history of slaves of African descent in the United States, the Civil War, and the Jim Crow laws all add credence to the contention that racism is deeply entrenched in the institutions of American culture. George Cunningham and Michael Sagas (2005) provide more evidence of racial inequality in sport with their suggestion of access discrimination in the promotion of African American men's college basketball coaches from assistant positions to head positions. These barriers that prohibit blacks from attaining coaching and leadership positions in sport can be in the form of social networking and norms that perpetuate the inaccessibility. For instance, in collegiate sport, many of the coaching positions are filled through a presumably formal process in which candidates submit their résumés and are chosen based on the required criteria and preferred criteria, which are usually stated in a position announcement and job description. While this process may seem formal and appear objective, there are informal practices that also take place. For instance, it is typical for rumors of positions that may be opening in the near future to be leaked before the official announcement. Therefore, if an individual does not have access to people in leadership positions, he or she would have no firsthand knowledge of open positions and already be at a disadvantage in preparing for the application process. Unofficial institutional practices and norms like these tend to disadvantage blacks and other minorities, considering that many of the upper managers, coaches, and leaders in sport are white men. Therefore, to be black and also a sexual minority would further intensify the difficulties of working or participating in sport.

Sexual Prejudice in Sport

Sexuality in sport is a topic that remains an anomaly. Sport in its modern competitive form was founded on the idea of building masculinity for boys. For instance, the Young Men's Christian Association (YMCA), founded in the late nineteenth century, was established to provide a positive masculine space for boys to follow traditional Christian beliefs. While advances have been made, sport remains regulated by strict gender roles, particularly regarding femininity. For instance, Nefertiti Walker, Trevor Bopp, and Michael Sagas (2011) found that society perceives sport to be a realm where masculine culture is the norm and femininity holds a place only in specifically women's sport. Therefore, anything less than hypermasculine cultural norms are perceived as inferior in sport (Walker and Bopp 2011).

There is very little research that examines the combined role of race and sexuality in sport. This is partly because there are very few instances in professional sport of black athletes coming out as gay until the early twenty-first century. For those who have come out, their sexual orientation has by no means been openly accepted by sport leagues and the media. Given the difficulties and lack of representation that blacks have had to face in sport, we would presume that black homosexuals would face even more prejudice.

There is little research directed at exploring the taboo topic of whether the black community supports black LGBT athletes. As Coretta Scott King, speaking at the National Black Leadership Commission on AIDS, said: "Homophobia is still a great problem throughout America, but in the African-American community it is even more threatening. . . . We have to launch a national campaign against homophobia in the Black community" (quoted in Lewis 2003:59). The black community as a whole, although quite disapproving of homosexual lifestyles, still does not agree with overt discrimination against sexual minorities. According to Gregory Lewis (2003), blacks' opinion on civil rights laws and employment discrimination are very similar to those of whites. Furthermore, blacks are supportive of laws prohibiting anti-gay discrimination. Thus, although the black community may disagree with the homosexual lifestyle, blacks still remain less likely than whites to contest civil rights for sexual minorities. Although the black community may support sexual minorities as a part of the civil rights agenda for all minorities, there remains little support for black sexual minorities as individuals within the African American community (Greene 2000). For black sexual minorities in sport, they may feel pressure from the African American community to conceal their sexual orientation because homosexuality is taboo among blacks. Also, for athletes in general, there is little support for revealing one's sexuality because of the hyper-masculine and heterosexual hegemony in sport.

Masculine Hegemony and Hegemonic Femininity

The term "hegemony" was coined by Antonio Gramsci (1971) to describe the economic and political strife occurring in Europe in the early 1970s. However, recent scholars have used the term to describe the inequalities in college sport (Norman 2010; Walker and Bopp 2011; Whisenant, Pedersen, and Obenour 2002). In sport, masculine hegemony can be described as taking place when society accepts the ruling of one group over another and the disenfranchised group knowingly and willingly accepts its place within the organization of sport. This notion of masculine hegemony aids in perpetuating the cycle of inequality in sport (Walker and Bopp 2011; Whisenant, Pedersen, and Obenour 2002). Masculine hegemony has been applied to recent research examining women who work in men's sport, who, like sexual minorities in sport, are marginalized (Walker and Bopp 2011). Nonetheless, results of this research suggest that the masculine hegemony present in men's sport supports a masculine domain in which anyone who may jeopardize the masculinity of the sport is denied access. The same is true for sport in general. Sport is a domain for reproducing masculinities. Therefore, nonheterosexual, nonmasculine culture is unwelcome in sport in general in the United States, but especially in men's sport.

Just as there is a hegemonic, privileged form of masculinity that dominates the sport culture, there is also a hegemonic form of femininity that dominates the sport world. Hegemonic femininity is an ideal or culturally accepted form of femininity that is white and heterosexual (Krane et al. 2004), and has strong connections to heterosexism in sport. Therefore, black lesbian athletes stand in stark contrast to the ideals of hegemonic femininity, which are reinforced through the media and society as whole (Krane et al. 2004). Again, similar to the tenets of masculine hegemony, hegemonic femininity is accepted and perpetuated not only by those it benefits (white, heterosexual men and women) but also by those it disenfranchises (nonwhite, homosexual men and women). Therefore, both of these frameworks act as barriers to LGBT people of color who wish to openly express their sexuality, while also adding to the prejudices they may endure.

Black Gay Men in Sport

As mentioned previously, blacks are overrepresented as players in certain sports—basketball and football. These sports tend to portray the highest levels of masculinity and physicality in sport culture in the United States. To the contrary, gay men are thought to participate in more feminine, nonaggressive sports such as ice skating, cheerleading, and gymnastics (Anderson 2005b). Because the differences between the two extremes are quite visible, people tend to develop stereotypes for each group over time: black men are hyper-masculinized and gay men are feminized by the sports they have been associated with. However, when paired, there is no stereotype that exists for the black gay male athlete: "Despite the gains of both the civil rights movement and the progress toward gay and lesbian social inclusion, the understanding in sport remains that Black athletes come in only one sexuality and gay men come in just one color" (Anderson and McCormack 2010a:146). This statement echoes the sentiment in sport that black men are hyper-masculine beings who play only competitive sports. To date in the United States, no black male athlete has come out as gay while still playing professional sport. Nor have any black male coaches come out as gay in the United States. Therefore, it is difficult for most observers to stereotype the black gay male athlete as playing a particular type of sport.

The fact that society cannot envision the existence of the black gay male athlete suggests that these athletes keep their sexual orientation deeply hidden within the realm of sport. Most of the recent literature on black gay men in sport suggests that while black heterosexual athletes are at the stage of perceived liberation, black gay athletes are still at the stage of contestation. According to the new social movement theory, black athletes are experiencing less overt discrimination and are culturally perceived as being equal to whites, whereas gay athletes are still seeking to obtain a voice in society and secure their civil liberties (Anderson and McCormack 2010a, 2010b). This is not to say that black male athletes are advantaged over their gay counterparts but to say that the two interrelated groups are at different stages of acceptance and visibility in sport.

The black community may be an added barrier that black gay athletes must deal with when coming out. For instance, Beverly Greene (2000) suggests that the conservative theological position of many African American churches, as well as the fear that homosexuality "threatens their chance at acceptance" into American culture, account for the lack of support many black LGBT individuals receive from the African American community. In a recent sport-related study, Richard Southall and colleagues (2011) found that black university athletes expressed higher rates of homophobia (sexual prejudice) than their white teammates. Likewise, data obtained from interviewing National Football League (NFL) rookies suggest that blacks are more likely to feel uncomfortable around gay teammates, and are also more likely to resort to physical violence if sexually propositioned by gay teammates (Ralph Cindrich cited in Anderson and McCormack 2010a).

Much of the research continues to support the notion that nonheterosexual behavior is less acceptable in the black community compared to the American population as a whole. Although some have suggested that the comparison of the black civil rights movement to the LGBT civil rights movement has little merit, the dynamics that result for those who are a member of both groups—men and women who are both black and gay—may prove more worthy of such comparisons. One concept that most researchers would agree on is that "racism and homophobia are similar, but also very different types of oppression. When they are combined, the collective experiences of denied citizenship are more extreme" (Kian and Anderson 2009:801). Again, this concept supports the notion that the sport environment, in its current form, may be too hostile an environment for black nonheterosexual athletes to comfortably express their sexuality within. This hostile environment perpetuates the cultural current norms that leave black gay athletes without a model for how, when, and where to come out in sport appropriately. Although John Amaechi has been presented as an example of a black gay professional athlete, he is British. So although he is a minority of color, he remains culturally different from African Americans.

Black Lesbian Women in Sport

Unlike their male counterparts, black lesbian athletes do have a model for coming out. As explored earlier, both Sheryl Swoopes and Kye Allums came out while still active as players in their respective leagues. Although Swoopes is now engaged to a man, she dated a woman for many years. But although Swoopes and Allums were able to come out while still active as athletes, both experienced short-lived careers after revealing their sexual identity. Though they both made the conscious decision to retire from their sport, their coming-out stories do not have the happy endings that many LGBT supporters may have hoped for. There is a host of literature supporting the notion that many lesbians who play or coach sport feel compelled to hide their sexual identity (Griffin 1992, 1998; Iannotta and Kane 2002; Krane and Barber 2005). When people compete for roles of leadership, such as head coach, sexuality has traditionally played a role in perceived ability to move up the professional ladder. Therefore, many sexual minorities have made the difficult decision to conceal their sexuality in order to avoid prejudice in the workplace. The results of a recent investigation into the experiences of lesbian intercollegiate coaches suggest that lesbian women in sport are faced with the task of constantly negotiating their identities of "coach" and "lesbian" (Krane and Barber 2005).

Research has also revealed that remaining silent is one way in which lesbian coaches deal with the often homophobic and heterosexist norms of college sport (Krane and Barber 2005). African American women in sport face unique difficulties and barriers that are unlike those experienced by their Caucasian female counterparts and African American male counterparts (Bruening 2005; McDowell and Cunningham 2009). Specifically, African American women, especially those in leadership positions, are more likely to make conscious efforts to adapt to and fit in with the social and cultural norms surrounding their sports (McDowell and Cunningham 2009). Therefore, African American lesbians may feel even less comfortable in sport given their multiple marginalized identities, none of which fit into the hyper-heterosexist norms of college sport. The sport in which black lesbian athletes have most recently announced their sexuality is basketball, which is the sport with the largest proportion of African American women participants (Zgonc 2010). In 2007–2008, black women comprised 50 percent of all NCAA Division I basketball players (DeHass 2009). However, during the same time frame, black women accounted for only 15 percent of head coaches in women's college basketball (Zgonc 2010). Based on the differences in these percentages, we can surmise that black women may be more comfortable expressing their sexual identity as players (e.g., Kye Allums and Sheryl Swoopes) than as coaches: to come out lesbian as a coach would add another marginalized identity. The phenomenon of black women openly expressing their sexual identity as athletes but not as coaches can be explained by addressing the intersectionality of race, gender, and sexuality. It is difficult enough for black women, who make up half the pool of athletes in college basketball, to get jobs as coaches.

Adding the additional barrier of nonheterosexuality only increases their struggle.

Intersectionality

Black LGBT individuals in sport have multiple minority identities. Not only are they usually visibly different from the majority of people in sport (white males), but they also must deal with having a sexual minority identity in an environment that is heterosexist and homophobic (Griffin 1998). Although visibly noticeable differences such as skin color allow society to easily label African Americans or blacks as the minority within sport, it is much more difficult to identify sexuality. Therefore, many LGBTs of color in sport are invisible. Most never come out and express their sexuality. However, this does not mean that they do not exist. LGBT individuals of color exist in sport, whether we can identify them or not. Therefore, they must constantly deal with the daunting task of negotiating the multiple identities.

Much of an LGBT individual's decision not to come out is influenced by intersectionality, the concept that forms of oppression are intensified when combined, such as for individuals who are both black and LGBT (Anderson and McCormack 2010a, 2010b; Crenshaw 1989, 1991). Keeping one of their oppressed identities hidden may be a mechanism that black LGBT athletes use to cope with the difficulties they face in sport, as well as reaffirm the marginalization of blacks. Indeed, the work of George Cunningham and John Singer (2010) suggests that black athletes have interest in attaining coaching positions but perceive the barriers to be too prohibitive. These barriers are even greater for black athletes who are LGBT, who must internalize the hiding of their lifestyle from teammates, coaches, and even their community. Therefore, many black LGBT athletes either leave their sport or community, or deny themselves the possibility of openly expressing their sexuality, both of which limit their liberty to live the open lives their white heterosexual counterparts experience.

Conclusion

Black LGBT individuals in sport remain an anomaly. As suggested by Eric Anderson and Mark McCormack: "Oppression of the openly gay male athlete remains so high that, in many circles, it is still common to hear explicit homophobic language and to witness clear homophobic discrimination that all too often goes unchallenged. It's obvious that overt, cultural, and institutional oppression of gay boys and men leads to more athletes remaining closeted compared to non-athletes" (2010b:959). The sport environment remains a breeding ground for sexual prejudice, which for black sexual minorities is magnified based on the historical struggle of African Americans in the United States. Therefore, the intersectionality of being both black and LGBT heightens the hostile environment of sport for these individuals. Despite progress in some segments of the entertainment industry and in the arts, particularly movies and music, sport appears resistant to addressing the plight of sexual minorities. Further, considering the historical significance of Jackie Robinson, Jesse Owens, and Wilma Rudolph for black athletes in general, black LGBT athletes are still waiting for their revolutionary leader to step forward.

Many would say that Sheryl Swoopes is such a leader, but with her recent engagement to a man, those who may not understand the continuum of sexuality are skeptical. Kye Allums's recent coming out as transsexual sets the tone for others to follow in her footsteps. However, despite her accomplishments as a college athlete, she is not as significant a model as the professional and Olympic-caliber athletes who are currently leading the way for black athletes. A black LGBT athlete who is accomplished and well-respected not only in a particular sport but also in the sport world as a whole is needed as a leader and role model.

More research into black LGBT sport figures is needed, whether examining coaches, players, or other sport professionals. Also critical is that this research be done from a variety of angles and sources. For instance, Anderson and McCormack (2010b) suggest using both intersectionality and critical race theory to analyze black LGBT athletes. This idea stems from the concept, present in both theories, that the voices of those who have experienced problems that are prevalent among multiple-minority individuals need to be heard. This research needs to examine the barriers that prevent black LGBT men and women from coming out, progressing in their profession, negotiating their identities, and surviving a life of secrecy in the world of sport.

According to the Movement Advancement Project (2012), increased media attention on incidents of suicide among LGBT youth has focused on the difficulty LGBT youth experience in being accepted among their peers, dealing with their sexuality, and lacking positive role models who have survived coming out. These same attributing factors are prevalent among black LGBT athletes. In order to be proactive in providing a safe space for these youth to participate in sport, more research needs to be done with LGBT athletes in general. Those researchers and stakeholders who may have roots in sport and may know LGBT athletes should act as gatekeepers into exploring the experiences of these athletes. Trusted gatekeepers must be established in the academic community if the voices of LGBT athletes, coaches, and sport officials are to be heard and their needs addressed with sensitivity and inclusion. Recent literature suggests that an organizational commitment to diversity in general and sexual orientation diversity in particular may go hand in hand with fostering a creative workplace (Cunningham 2011b). Therefore, the presence of people who are both sexually diverse and racially diverse may be particularly beneficial to the overall well-being of an organization.

It is important that sport managers, researchers, and others who hold interest in sport focus on inclusivity and sensitivity in addressing the needs of diverse individuals. Sexuality is not always revealed by the way people dress, talk, or present themselves. Just because the black LGBT athlete has not been stereotyped in the media does not mean that such an individual does not exist. In studying racial and sexual minorities, it is important to understand the intersectionality that exists among these individuals and their identities. They must deal not only with the racial issues present in the United States but also with the lack of acceptance for sexually diverse individuals. Their struggles against underrepresentation, access barriers, and institutionalized bias stem not simply from being black but from being black and LGBT. These multiple identities come with multiple sources of prejudice.

6

The Gay Games

Caroline Symons

The founder of the Gay Games, Tom Waddell, was highly critical of what he saw as the elitist, racist, sexist, ageist, homophobic, nationalistic, and overly commercial Olympics and professional sport movement. One of his main visions for the Gay Games was to "raise consciousness and enlighten people outside of the gay community, but within the gay community as well" (quoted in Messner 1994: 119). Through the Gay Games, people would be brought together to engage in a sport festival based on the principles of participation, inclusion, and doing one's personal best. Waddell described his vision thus:

> We have age-group competitions, so all ages can be involved. We have parity—if there's a men's sport, there's a women's sport to complement it. And we go out and recruit in Third World and minority areas. All of these people are going to get together for a week, they're gonna march in together, march out together, they're gonna hold hands, and they'll say: This is wonderful! There's this discovery. . . . Everybody's welcome! Let's get together and have a festival—a people's Games. (quoted in Messner 1994:119)

The first Gay Games were held in the lesbian and gay haven of San Francisco in 1982 (Gay Games I), organized by a small group of volunteers and involving 1,300 athletes from eleven Western countries. Many lesbians and gays were publicly visible for the first time.

They could engage in their sporting passions and meet others with similar interests in an environment of encouragement and celebration. This can be seen as marking a shift in gay liberation from concentrating on the politics of oppression to focusing more positively and publicly on expressing gay identity and pride (Pronger 1990: 251). The organizers also envisaged the Games as an important vehicle for bringing together the diverse gay and lesbian community, and especially the separate men's and women's communities of the time, through the commonality of sport (Symons 2010:45–47).

The Gay Games have become one of the largest quadrennial international lesbian, gay, bisexual, and transgender (LGBT) events. Subsequent Gay Games were held in San Francisco (Gay Games II, 1986), Vancouver (Gay Games III, 1990), New York (Gay Games IV, 1994), Amsterdam (Gay Games V, 1998), Sydney (Gay Games VI, 2002), Chicago (Gay Games VII, 2006), and Cologne (Gay Games VIII, 2010), and by the time of the 1994 New York Games, participants numbered over 10,000, hailing from all continents and encompassing the rich diversity of LGBT communities. This chapter explores the meaning and significance of the Gay Games for community-making in LGBT sport and culture. It examines conceptual notions of community and presents a brief historical overview of the Gay Games up until the Chicago Games of 2006. The impact on community of the divisive split in the international LGBT sport movement that occurred in 2004 and the "lived" experience of organizers and participants of the Gay Games are explored.

This chapter is based on the ethnographic materials that informed a comprehensive social history of the Gay Games (Symons 2010), including semistructured in-depth interviews of key organizers as well as participants of Gay Games I–VII, archival materials, participant observation, and extensive secondary sources.[1] Interviews included people from the United States, Canada, the Netherlands, England, Germany, South Africa, and Australia. Priority was given to the key shapers of the Games, although many organizers have also been sport and cultural participants, coaches, and spectators.[2] Diverse voices encompassing different sexual orientations, races, ethnicities, ages, classes, genders, political perspectives, and abilities were sought; however, the majority of those interviewed described themselves as white, lesbian or gay, and middle class, and were between twenty-four and eighty-two years old and had completed tertiary education. Many interviewees were from the United States, reflecting the origins and place of multiple hosting of the Gay Games.

Defining Community

The term "community" is one of the keywords that we all use "when we wish to discuss many of the central processes of our common life" (Williams 1985:14). Sociologists have concentrated on community as a geographic locale where people live, but with the more fluid movement of people across cities and countries brought about by migration, shifting work, and settlement patterns across a lifetime, greater emphasis has been placed on shared social systems. The content and quality of these social relationships and meanings involve understanding "community" as a sense of identity or belonging. Such subjective interpretations focus on issues of meaning and feeling and a sense of "communion." When these meanings and feelings are shared significantly, they express a shared culture. Clifford Geertz (1973) defines culture as "the webs of significance" spun by people to make sense of the world and give meaning to their lives. The shared stories, symbols, belief systems, and important events are all part of these webs of significance.

Academic and gay rights activist Dennis Altman favors this more subjective perspective of community. It is self-defined or imagined by its members, in which the groups of people involved "feel enough in common for whatever reason to share common aspirations, goals and institutions" (1994:15). B. Anderson, in his provocative study *Imagined Communities,* saw "deep, horizontal comradeship" as essential to communities and conceptualized modern nationhood itself as imagined because "the members of even the smallest nation will never know most of their fellow-members, meet them, or even hear of them, yet in the minds of each lives the image of their communion" (1983:6). Communion is also achieved through the creation of the "other" as a common enemy or threat challenging the community. By coming together against this "common enemy," community can be reinvigorated and reinforced (Anderson 1983:7). Certainly the LGBT community has been regarded as the "other" in many countries, and being "othered" has provided an important wellspring for its identity and formation.

Community is also cultivated by the communal imagining portrayed in the mass media and most recently by the widespread and global adoption of online media and the information and communication networks that have produced new, virtual communities. The LGBT media are central networks of information, communication, and community-shaping locally and internationally, and have been an integral part of the Gay Games.

The LGBT community that takes part in the Gay Games is diverse, encompassing lesbians, gay men, bisexuals, transfolk, and queers from many different racial, ethnic, socioeconomic, differently abled, political, and national backgrounds. There are significant differences in economic and social power, as well as gendered cultural perspectives among gays and lesbians, differences that can become political and divisive. Transgender people also have an ambivalent relationship within the lesbian and gay community (Couch et al. 2007). There is no single outlook among the transgender community either (Califia 1997:chaps. 1, 5; Symons and Hemphill 2006:109–115). Lesbian feminists who emphasize the importance of women's culture and the impact of patriarchal oppression have been opposed to the inclusion of those not born "womyn" in their community-making (Califia 1997:106–107; Symons 2004:432–433). The gendered and sexually different—othered—status of transgender individuals has been the common ground engaging them within the broader gay community.

In addition to these many differences, there are also strong commonalities that enable LGBT community formation. Altman observed that shared sexuality can be the basis for strong connections and a real sense of belonging (Altman 1994). The common goals and aspirations of sexual minorities in most Western countries, such as acquiring legal and political rights and relationship equality, and ending social discrimination and homophobic violence, have forged community connections and solidarity, established political and social organizations, and enabled communal imaginings. Furthermore, many metropolitan cities have thriving gay and lesbian communities with gay-run media, commercial and social life, celebratory art, and cultural events including sport.

Charles Arcordia and Michelle Whitford (2008) discuss the important contribution that participation in festivals such as the Sydney Gay and Lesbian Mardi Gras makes to building the bedrock of shared community imaginings, cohesion, and the enabling of networks and resources—social capital—for the Sydney LGBT community. Volunteer and paid organizers of this event develop expertise, interact and forge stronger links with local LGBT and mainstream businesses and community organizations, and raise awareness about this expertise and community capacity. Social, support, and business networks can develop well beyond a single event, and if this is a reoccurring event, these networks can be further developed and sustained. Social cohesion and the sharing of a worldview are also enacted through events such as the Mardi Gras, where the main purpose is to be public, visible, and proud as LGBT, while at the same time focusing on celebration, fun, education, politics, and social and political reform (Carbery 1995:5–6). The celebratory nature of events such as the Mardi Gras also generate feelings of goodwill and "communitas" (Salamone 2000). There are strong parallels in the dynamics of community-making through the Mardi Gras and the Gay Games.

A Brief Community History of the Gay Games

While inclusivity was central to the first Gay Games, this event also had a strong mainstreaming or normalizing purpose. All sports events were encouraged to gain official sanctioning by mainstream sporting bodies, and the opening and closing ceremonies were based on Olympic tradition, including the marching of athletes in their sports uniforms. Aligned to this normalization was censorship of the lesbian and gay community's more radical and flamboyant elements, as drag and leather were deemed inappropriate at the first and second Gay Games (Symons 2010:41–44). All the respondents I interviewed who had been to the first two Games reported feeling affirmed as gay and lesbian sportspeople, and recognized the pioneering contribution of these Games.[3]

The Gay Games II were more international (nineteen countries represented) and diverse in program offering, with seventeen sports events and a small cultural festival staged, the latter involving performances from massed brass bands and choruses. The cultural festival was based on communal activities that, along with sport club involvement, promoted social connections, relationships of shared interest, skill development, reciprocity, support, and mutual achievement (R. Mitchell, interview, November 16, 1996; M. Clarke, interview, November 26, 1996). At the time of these Gay Games, San Francisco was the epicenter of the HIV/AIDS crisis in the United States. Organizers envisaged these Games as being an important vehicle for individual and community health promotion (S. Kelly, interview, November 13, 1996; Symons 2010:78–80).

The third Gay Games were held outside the United States in nearby Vancouver (1990). Over 7,500 athletes and 2,000 cultural participants from thirty nations attended these Games. Due to their increased size and scope, it was necessary to employ a small event-management team to oversee the Games. The bulk of the event work was still performed by a large group of volunteers. The Gay Games III can be viewed as transitional—from the local to the global dimensions of future Games (Symons 2010:100–119).

The Gay Games IV were held in the one of the media and commercial capitals of the world, New York City, and the organizers set out to make them the biggest, most visible and diverse, celebrity enhanced, and professionally conducted Games so far. There were 15,000 sport and cultural participants hailing from forty-five countries spanning six continents, engaged in 31 sport events and 130 cultural exhibitions and performances (Labreque 1994). The event budget totaled $6.5 million, with an economic impact estimated at $100 million (City of New York 1996). Over 6,000 volunteers, many from the local LGBT community, were involved in the planning and staging of these Games. A network of community-based committees drove the event, and the 31 sport events were organized by gay and lesbian–identified sport clubs working in partnership with mainstream sport organizations. There was also a team of paid staff who covered all event-management aspects, enriching their expertise and enabling important commercial, political, and civic connections within the LGBT community of New York as well as with the broader establishment (Unity '94 1994b; R. Quarto, interview, December 1–2, 1996). The latter included securing substantial sponsorship based on the supposed lucrative "pink" dollar and the cultivation of excellent working relations with the New York mayor's office, police department, and transport authorities (Unity '94 1994b).

Queer culture was celebrated in the ceremonies and cultural festival. Drag queens carried the city and country signs preceding each sport team that marched in the opening ceremony. Participation by transgender folk was recognized and enabled by the first Gay Games transgender policy (Gay Games IV and Cultural Festival 1994). Queer sport and cultural icons such as Greg Louganis, Martina Navratilova, Bruce Hayes, Billie Jean King, Sir Ian McKellen, Bill T. Jones, and Sandra Bernhart were featured at the Games to boost their profile and raise funding. Games organizers secured excellent media coverage from the international gay press and front-page coverage in the *New York Times,* ensuring the main stories and meanings of the Gay Games were shared widely (Symons 2010:127–130). The Gay Games IV were a major success, having significant economic and social impact, including LGBT community development.

The Gay Games V were held outside North America, a first, in arguably the most gay-friendly city and country in the world—

Amsterdam, the Netherlands. The Games recorded 15,000 participants, coming from forty nations, with half from Europe, involved in thirty sports, as well as an extensive program of cultural and social issues, including human rights (Stichting Gay and Lesbian Games 1998). This old-world walking city was remade as festive and gay for the duration of the Games. LGBT diversity was embraced and the boundaries of community-making were extended at these Games, facilitated by outreach programs concentrating on equalizing women's participation and integrating people with disabilities as well as lesbians and gays living in Eastern Europe and former colonies of the Netherlands (Stichting Gay and Lesbian Games 1998; van Leewen 1998). A program of storytelling and social issues was an innovation of these Games, involving LGBT people from all over the world in a forum where they could share their cultural background, personal stories, and human rights challenges (Symons 2010:157–161). For the first time, non-Western LGBT identities and perspectives were given a voice and place at the Gay Games.

The Gay Games VI, the first to be held in the Southern Hemisphere, in Sydney in 2002, extended this global diversity and community-making even further. The Sydney Games included indigenous peoples, especially from the Asia Pacific region, and their different Western and non-Western ways of conceptualizing and living gender and sexuality (Symons 2010:192–195). According to the Gay Games VI participation policy, gender was defined as a social identity, enabling numerous indigenous transgender teams from across the Pacific to play in the netball and volleyball competitions of these Games (Sydney Games 2002b; Borrie 2003:112–113). Conceptualizations of gender, as well as rule-making and organization in netball to ensure fairness, safety, and LGBT community formation within teams, were adaptive and flexible at these Games (C. Mueller, interview, February 19, 2003).[4] A number of community-based committees working within the Sydney Games provided direction and management of a scholarship program (180 committees in total) that enabled the inclusion of indigenous Australians and Pacific Islanders.

It could be argued that the impact of these diversity programs, while important, was still minimal, as the majority of participants at the Sydney Games were relatively affluent white gay men and to a lesser extent lesbians from North America, Europe, and Australia; only 5.5 percent of participants were from the Asia Pacific region (excluding Australia, from which 25.3 percent of participants originated) (Borrie 2003:63–64).[5] This affluent Western gay demographic was the focus of the marketing, sponsorship, and programming of the Gay Games, and Western understandings of (homo)sexual identity politics were also explicitly celebrated through this out-and-proud major public event (Waitt 2006).

The sport program of the Sydney Games was particularly well organized, with the majority of the thirty-one sports being staged in effective working partnerships between local LGBT-identified sport clubs and their respective state and national sport bodies. LGBT sport organizers (all of them volunteers) from these clubs received training covering customer service, cross-cultural and disability awareness, and venue, event, and job-specific training for the particular role they played in organizing the sport events (Borrie 2003:70–73). LGBT community development and capacity building, particularly in the area of event management, and the forging of useful sport networks were enabled through the initiatives and experiences of these Games. The professionalism and friendliness of the Games were highlighted by a veteran Gay Games participant and organizer, Des Sullivan: "The sport was very well organized. The city was wonderful. The participants enjoyed themselves and they all wanted to go to another Gay Games" (interview, February 20, 2003). Sullivan also commented on the bridge-building between the gay and lesbian community and mainstream sport organizations and communities that occurred at the Sydney Games. He had observed of the officials at the track and field competition, "who probably never dealt with or had contact with gay and lesbian people, in a positive way anyway, how quickly they bonded and became good friends." He also remarked on the appreciation some of these top Australian officials had for the standard of athleticism of the gay and lesbian sprinters, some of whom were Olympians. One of the officials who had initially been quite aggressive at the meet joined in with the camaraderie and humor that prevailed among the officials and organizers. Another official experienced homophobic disapproval from her daughter over her volunteering for the Games, but she countered the negative stereotypes of gay people expressed by her daughter with the real-life experiences she had with gay and lesbian athletes and event volunteers. Tim Fisher, the venue manager for the tennis competition at the Sydney Games, reflected on the bridge-building capacity of the Games:

> One of the unwritten successes I believe of the Gay Games was the changing of attitude many people had towards gay and lesbian peo-

ple. When I first went to Cintra Park the two guys that helped run it
were cold, distant and even disdainful of me and the Games. At the
end of the Games they were happy, joking with me and coming to
ask all sorts of questions (on which I was able to educate them) and
often came to talk to me in the control desk. It was a great shift for
them. (Borrie 2003:7)

There are numerous accounts of these positive bridge-building impacts made through social interaction facilitated by the sharing of
common sporting demands and passions at the Gay Games (Symons
2010:188–189). The Gay Games have developed sporting communities, networks, and capacities for LGBT people involved in the organization and participation of the event. Challenging homophobia
and building networks within mainstream sport are important outcomes of the Gay Games.

The celebration and affirmation of queer sporting culture is another important outcome and was featured strongly in the sport and
culture program of the Sydney Games. For instance, there was the
Grand Ball, billed as a "fairy-tale night of colour and indulgence for
all queer Princes and Princesses assembled to celebrate the conclusion
of the Dancing Competition"; the Oceania Pacific Paradise Party,
which evoked images of the South Pacific in the Sydney Aquatic Centre for all swimmers, divers, and water polo competitors to celebrate
at the end of their events; and the Cool on Ice spectacular, which featured the best individual and same-sex couple performances on ice
(Sydney Games 2002a:21). Gender and sexual identities were explored, and the aesthetic and often irreverent queer cultures took center stage for the pleasure of Gay Games participants and spectators, as
well as to increase the commercial viability of the Games.

The Sydney Games are also well remembered for their major financial deficit, which caused significant community divisiveness and
financial pain. Smaller businesses that had not been paid for services
rendered to stage the Games were especially affected, and trust in
participation in gay events was undermined. The dominant image of
the Games was one of mismanagement (Farrar 2002). The budgetary
uncertainty that beset these Games had other negative impacts, including a stressful working environment in which the various departments that organized the Games had to compete for scarce resources,
as well as burnout among workers and volunteers and an inability to
celebrate the organizational achievements of the Games when faced
with such issues (Symons 2010:196–198).

The Sydney Games of 2002 were not the first Gay Games to have a substantial deficit,[6] and the overseeing body of the Gay Games—the Federation of Gay Games—became increasingly concerned over the negative impact these financial difficulties were having on the Gay Games brand. By 2003 the federation had taken a conservative turn, advocating the downscaling of the Games and budgetary prudence. This occurred during the contract negotiations for the Gay Games VII, which had been awarded to Montreal after its very ambitious bid to host the Games of 2006—projected to be twice as big as any previously held. The scene was set for a major split in the international LGBT sport movement, with the Gay Games VII eventually being held in Chicago, and with Montreal organizing the first World Outgames, which took place two weeks after the Chicago Gay Games and one hour's plane flight away (Symons 2010:218–223).

Divisions Within International LGBT Sporting Communities

The split over the Gay Games VII took on geopolitical divisions and spawned a rival international body, the Gay and Lesbian International Sport Association (GLISA). The Gay Games VII in Chicago were essentially American, with 9,288 of their 12,000 participants coming from the United States and only 2,500 coming from sixty-nine other countries. Missing from these Games was the diversity seen in the past (Buzinski 2006). Montreal's subsequent World Outgames attracted a record Canadian attendance (Canadians made up 39 percent of 12,000 participants) as well as participation from 111 countries, the main ones being the United States (19 percent), Germany (7 percent), the Netherlands, Australia, and France (6 percent each), and the United Kingdom (5 percent) (DGQ Media Inc. 2006). LGBT national loyalties and imaginings were at play in the taking of sides and participation at these two queer gaming venues.

This community divisiveness has had its opportunities as well as threats. For instance, the total number of people who attended both the Gay Games VII in Chicago and the World Outgames in Montreal represented a near doubling of attendance at past Gay Games, and there was also an increase in program choice, including opportunities to be involved in the largest LGBT international human rights conference to be held so far (DGQ Media Inc. 2006). GLISA has also introduced regional Games in between the international major Games events that take place every four years.[7] In 2008 the first Asia Pacific Outgames were successfully held in Melbourne, and these were followed by the second Asia Pacific Outgames in Wellington in 2011. The regional Games may be more accessible financially and logistically for some, and the Asia Pacific Games have also built LGBT community capacity within the host cities (Melbourne Outgames Inc. 2008; Asia Pacific Games 2011).

The threats from this international divisiveness concern sustainability and community cohesion. For instance, there was a reduction in overall participant numbers in the World Outgames held in Copenhagen and Cologne, and securing sponsorship was a challenge especially with the Gay Games VIII.[8] The Berlin LGBT community's sport organization—Team Berlin—questioned this sustainability as well as the divisive impact on Games attendees in a thirty-foot-long petition presented to the Federation of Gay Games and GLISA in September 2009. Team Berlin called for a return to the original vision of the Gay Games, that of community unity, pride, and the furthering of human rights. It also lamented the divisive impact of the split on the worldwide gay and lesbian sport movement and advocated for a more active and effective reconciliation process between GLISA and the Federation of Gay Games, and the staging of one international LGBT gaming venue (Team Berlin 2009).

Experiencing Community Through the Gay Games

This brief history of the Gay Games has highlighted their progressively inclusive, community, and capacity-building strengths and divisions. I now turn to the lived experience of community among both the organizers and participants. This lived experience will allow us to appreciate the wellsprings of community and identity, and the webs of meaning and significance, generated from the Gay Games.

Unity and Diversity

A strong theme that emerged from the interviews was the feeling of unity and communion experienced during the Gay Games. Participants stressed their sense of being welcomed, accepted, and affirmed. James, a white gay male in his early forties who had lived in many parts of the United States as a son of a naval officer, told me that he felt disillusioned by the discrimination within the gay and lesbian community. James had competed in weightlifting at the Gay Games IV and, as a big man, found it difficult to fit into what he identified as a youthful, beautiful body–obsessed gay male culture where he lived in San Francisco:

> The Gay Games has helped me to be very proud of the fact that I'm a gay man. And I mean it's done a lot of healing for me. . . . Because sometimes I get in a space, walking into the Castro I am ashamed of being gay because of the cruelty we show each other about looks, attitude, dress, men not liking women, women not liking men, age, lookism, you know the whole thing. (interview, November 20, 1996)

He found the Gay Games a much more inclusive culture:

> The attitude goes away and we are really united. You're there celebrating each other. There is respect. There was respect for women, women were respecting men, there wasn't any separatism, it was just wonderful. . . . [W]ith AIDS going around there's a lot of sadness and it's obvious. People being gone, things stopped. Not in the Gay Games. You feel the joy; it was amazing to feel the joy coming out of the people. It was like an energy, a really wonderful energy. (interview, November 20, 1996)

Another gay male, Greg, who had lived in South Africa (of English descent) for most of his life, had returned to his sport of competitive swimming in his thirties when he joined the London gay and lesbian team Out To Swim. Greg felt welcomed and free to express himself at the Gay Games:

> It means a place where I know I will be welcome. It means a sport arena, a swimming pool where I know I will be welcome. Where my sexuality will no longer get in the way of my performance, my best, where I can meet other sportsmen and women who share the same strangeness with me, whatever that strangeness may be . . . it's about change, it's about acknowledging difference, it's about expressing ourselves, being me. (interview, December 13, 1996)

Roz, a twenty-nine-year-old lesbian woman from New York, of Polish, Italian, and Jewish descent, who played softball during the Gay Games III in Vancouver (and was also an organizer of the Gay Games IV), relished her experiences of unity and community:

I mean we took over Vancouver. I met gays and lesbians from all over the world, we played softball against a bunch of people from Salt Lake City, Utah. I thought that there were only Mormons in Salt Lake; it never occurred to me that there were dykes who played softball in Salt Lake and drank beer. Never mind everyone we met from Germany and everywhere else, [so] you don't feel isolated. And then personally for me I watched thirteen women play better individually and as a team than they ever had done in their lives. (interview, December 2, 1996)

In a study using social identity theory as a foundation, Vikki Krane, Heather Barber, and Lisa McClung investigated the impact of Gay Games participation on social identity, self-esteem, and collective self-esteem as well as "expected subsequent social change activities following the Games." An open-ended questionnaire was given to 125 lesbian and bisexual athletes from eleven countries who had attended the Gay Games V. One of the main themes to emerge from this study was the enhancement of social identity as LGBT through Gay Games involvement. New knowledge was gained about the LGBT community—it was large, international, and diverse—and this was viewed very positively (2002: 27, 34).

Visibility, Celebration, and Empowerment

Many Gay Games participants recalled their feelings of affirmation and empowerment from being so visible and celebrating LGBT culture, sport, and community at the Gay Games. Central to this empowerment was the warm welcome received by host cities, and the abiding sense that the lesbian and gay community had taken over those cities during the Games. This is a unique experience for LGBT people, considering their experience of discrimination, marginalization, and invisibility through pervasive societal heterosexism and homophobic stigma. A thirty-year-old white lesbian soccer player from Ireland named Heather summarized this empowerment thus:

But being in New York with the Gay Games crowd was just like being in a gay city, it was amazing. . . . It was like everywhere you went there were lesbians and gays everywhere, it was just a perpetual high, you know . . . it was quite a long tube journey from where we were staying [to where they played soccer]. And out to all of our games we'd be singing and dancing in the tube carriage and all the

people reacted quite differently, like straight American people,
reacted quite differently to what we'd here [in London]. But they
all ended up clapping us along and cheering us. (interview,
December 12, 1996)

In a similar way, Roz recalled "taking over" Vancouver during Gay
Games II: "The city is small and it was like gays had taken over the
whole city and everyone was gay" (interview, December 2, 1996).

But arguably it was Amsterdam, as a relatively compact "old-
world" walking city, that was most "taken over" by the Gay Games.
In fact, the main cultural and sport sites of these Games (with the exception of the swimming pool) were all centrally located and accessible on foot or by public transport. The city center was decorated
with Gay Games signage and symbols, and the national flags that
fluttered from buildings throughout the city displayed pink colors in
replacement of red or green. There were queer-themed art exhibitions
in the galleries, and outdoor queer film, music, and choir festivals in
the main city squares. A Friendship Village was established next to
the Town Hall and was surrounded by an outdoor entertainment area
on the banks of the Amstel River (Stichting Gay and Lesbian Games
1998:6; Symons 2010:150). Mainstream and gay media covered the
Games extensively. Opening and closing ceremonies of the Games
were held in Ajax Stadium and featured a parade of Games athletes
and cultural festival participants marching under the banners of their
city and country; gay, lesbian, and transgender celebrity performers
and LGBT-themed performances; as well as speeches evoking LGBT
pride and celebration in front of a cheering, predominantly LGBT audience alongside city and country dignitaries such as the major of
Amsterdam and the prime minister of the Netherlands. Visibility,
pride, celebration, and empowerment were strong features of these
Gay Games experiences. LGBT people were the affirmed majority,
and their sporting and cultural achievements, their human rights, and
their community making were center stage.

In one study of 1994 Gay Games participants the females interviewed "expressed the importance of participation in an inclusive
sport environment, feelings of self-enhancement and empowerment,
and the social and political importance of participating in the Gay
Games." The two most important motives for their involvement with
the Gay Games were "being with other LGBT athletes and for the
sense of community the Games provided" (Krane and Romont,
1997:136). My colleagues and I (Symons et al. 2010:36–38) noted

that some of the most positive and affirming experiences of sport reported by LGBT people from Australia centered on their sense of community and empowerment at the Sydney Gay Games. Krane, Barber, and McClung (2002:38), in their study of Gay Games V participants, found that the Games, by emphasizing positive LGBT identities, also enhanced collective self-esteem. This was particularly salient for people with marginalized social identities, and community pride and empowerment were also found to be strong drivers for social change such as coming out to family and friends and becoming more active with LGBT social justice issues.

A Significant Life Experience

Through my research on the history of the Gay Games, I came across numerous accounts of participants and organizers being inspired and transformed in various ways through their experience of the Games. For Gene, a wrestler of Irish Italian descent who grew up in New Jersey, the Gay Games provided him with a sport and social world that he had yearned for since high school: "It was the best [Gay] Games [San Francisco] in terms of how it changed my life. I got there, ah, and realized that I was not the only one who was gay, who was not the only one who was involved in wrestling on a 'legitimate' level—coaching, participating, had a life—but met other men who were into the same kind of thing" (interview, November 22, 1996). Gene moved to San Francisco after the first Games and became one of the key organizers and coaches of the most successful wrestling clubs in the country. He has served on the Federation of Gay Games for many years as well.

Roz described the Gay Games III as the "most empowering ten days of my life" (interview, December 2, 1996). The games thus helped her overcome many barriers and stereotypes she held about the gay community. She changed political allegiance (became less conservative), gained confidence in being open about her sexuality at work, and even convinced her parents to join her in the New York Pride Parade.

Kate, an Australian of English descent, was in her fifties when I interviewed her in Sydney just after the Gay Games VI. Heavily involved in the lesbian feminist movement during the 1980s, she had turned her energies to elite masters cycling and the development of the gay and lesbian sport movement locally and internationally after being inspired through her Gay Games IV experience: "Gay Games

IV changed my life. . . . I just felt part of this amazing global event and I met people that I'm still in contact with." In response to my follow-up question, "How did the Games change your life?" Kate said: "Well I think it did something for my self-esteem. About being proud about who I am, particularly my sexuality, and I don't have to do endless amounts of political work to feel it [is] okay to be a lesbian, which I have done for years" (interview, February 16, 2003).

Stuart, a forty-something white gay New Zealander living in Australia, discussed being a private person, especially in terms of his sexuality and openness. His first involvement with the gay and lesbian community occurred in his thirties when he got involved with the Sydney Frontrunners and volunteered as a counselor on the local gay and lesbian switchboard. Like Roz, Stuart attended the Gay Games IV as a Frontrunner and described his Games experience thus:

> It was just a really mind-blowing experience. I'd run with the Frontrunners on local runs in Sydney but there was always this being on guard about my ways of behaving publicly . . . but [the] New York Games was my first experience where I felt free to be myself in sport. To embrace, hug, kiss, to be tactile with friends that I knew very well and in a sport environment which was very different to what I'd experienced previously in my life. . . . Marching into Yankee Stadium with something like 50,000 people at the closing ceremony for New York, I almost burst into tears, I felt that every single goose bump on my body was about to explode because it was an incredible, proud moment. (interview, May 12, 2003)

Stuart was the director of sport for the Gay Games VI and has gone on to become a national and international (mainstream) sport administrator.

Bondyopadhyay had traveled from India to Australia to participate in the first International Sport and Human Rights conference held in Sydney during the Gay Games VI. Being openly gay and working for gay rights in India was challenging for Bondyopadhyay, and while he was inspired by the Gay Games, he was also "poignantly reminded of the complexities and hardships of seeking universal rights and freedoms based on a gay sexual identity":

> I could see the distance we have to travel back home before we get to a point of celebrating our sexuality without fear or repression. I could also feel the euphoria of freedom where it exists, and the desirability for it, for it is inherently good. But most of all I could

feel a validation of what I do back home, for unfolding before my eyes was an ideal that could be had, and playing in the back of my mind was the actual oppression I witnessed every day . . . in India. (Bondyopadhyay 2002)

Tracy Baim, who oversaw the outreach and scholarship program that enabled 120 athletes from across the world to attend the Gay Games VII, reflected in an interview that the highlight of the Games for her was witnessing the positive impact they had on scholarship recipients. She recalled this impact on the captain of the Chosen Few, the South African women's soccer team:

I visited . . . the captain of the team, who lives in horrible conditions in Soweto, and I said to her, five to six months after the Games, "Did it mean anything to you?" and she said, "I will always have Chicago." That sentence meant everything to me, all the things we worked for, all the hard board meetings, et cetera, it was made worthwhile because she will always have Chicago. She went on to say, "We felt like queens for a week and were treated like human beings for a week." She and her team won the bronze medal in the B division of women's soccer. They would have loved to have won gold, but they won through their participation in Chicago. (interview, October 27, 2007)

AIDS, Commemoration, and Health-Making

A recurring theme that emerged from the history of the Gay Games II–IV was the sadness within the community brought by the death of friends, loved ones, community workers, and leaders by the onslaught of AIDS.[9] The Gay Games provided an important antidote to this sadness. Roz captured this perspective in remembering the Gay Games III: "You know, we are in a community that because of AIDS doesn't celebrate much any more, and [the Gay Games offered] pure and total celebration, and [life outside the Games is not] like that" (interview, December 2, 1996). The Gay Games II were organized during the height of the AIDS epidemic in San Francisco and many within the local community thought the Games were an extravagance that took human and financial resources away from managing the medical and community crisis and presented dangers of further contagion.

The executive director of the Gay Games II, Shawn Kelly, expressed a more positive perspective, advocating opportunities to promote self-esteem, community connections and support, and healthy lifestyles (including some of the first safe-sex campaigns) through sport and cultural participation. For Kelly "the Gay Games were the antithesis of the AIDS crisis. In many respects our community needs a psychological boost and the Games would provide it" (quoted in Coe 1986:14). Tom Waddell discussed the Games in the local gay press as a vehicle "in which gay men and lesbian women could demonstrate their productive, creative, multi-faceted and thus healthy culture" (1986:8). He stated that in such challenging times, health could be promoted through engaging in sensible exercise and sport, positive social connections, the development of support networks, resilience, and the furthering of community capacities within local gay and lesbian populations. For Waddell, raising esteem within individuals and communities was central to this health promotion.

Gary Reece, a Texas-based writer, academic, and cyclist, reflected on the emotional impact of the New York Games ceremonies, in which he was able to simultaneously celebrate life and LGBT community while also remembering those who had died:

> The Ceremonies made me feel so proud: they brought tears to my eyes and sent shivers down my spine. They were a time to remember the dead and a time to honour the living—to hold both at the same moment. The Games offered a rare chance to simultaneously celebrate our lives and mourn our losses. For once I did not feel the push-pull of trying to do one without the other, as if we have to isolate AIDS and everything it means to us before we can began to feel good about ourselves, and our future. (quoted in Labreque 1994: 78–79)

The Gay Games IV mounted a dedicated campaign to promote positive images of people living with HIV and AIDS (Symons 2010: 85–86), and organizers worked hard to welcome people with different needs, including those with "accessibility and mobility problems, neurological disorders, psychological problems, chemical sensitivity, cognitive problems" as well as those living with HIV and AIDS (Unity '94 1994b). This was achieved through comprehensive policy, staff training, and disability service provision (Weinberg 1994; Symons 2010:86–87).

Diverse Sporting Communities

In over half of the more than thirty interviews I conducted with gay men involved in the Gay Games, interviewees recalled alienating and negative experiences with sport during their formative years and only returned to subsequent games with the advent of gay sports organizations and events. My colleagues and I (Symons et al. 2010) found that 42 percent of the 308 participants we surveyed in our comprehensive study of the LGBT sport experience in Victoria, Australia, had suffered homophobic verbal abuse and 46 percent kept their sexuality hidden from everyone in their mainstream sport club. Though the nature, extent, and impact of sexual and gender prejudice in sport vary worldwide, with more prejudice experienced in rural areas than in cosmopolitan cities, prejudice in the West has diminished over the past three decades. Agnes Ellings, Paul De Knop, and Annelies Knoppers (2003) found that in one of the most gay-tolerant nations of the world—the Netherlands—the pull factors of belonging, self-esteem, and affirmation that characterized the experiences of lesbians and gays in LGBT-identified sports clubs were stronger than the push factors of sexual discrimination. LGBT-identified sport clubs, organizations, and events have formed within the broader context of gay identity and rights politics and greater acceptance of gay people within society in general. The development of gay and lesbian sport has also been shaped by the growth of the international LGBT sport movement, and the Gay Games have played a preeminent role in this process. It is at the local club level that community-making is most salient on a day-to-day basis, and there are diverse sporting communities that make up the Gay Games experience.

Terry, a forty-year-old Anglo-American living in San Diego, swam in the very first Gay Games, as well as in subsequent Games. Terry had coached and swum with the gay swim team in San Diego, and had represented the International Gay and Lesbian Aquatics (IGLA) at the Federation of Gay Games. Terry acknowledged the significance of homophobia in sport and the inclusive and affirming environment the Gay Games provided for LGBT people. He also emphasized the opportunities the Games provided for breaking down stereotypes for gay men in sport. The centrality of sport, and the diversity of the sports played at the Gay Games, including those of a more "macho" variety like football and ice hockey, give gay men of all types (butch, tough, gentle, queeny) and sporting interests a chance to participate and compete. Terry had more to say on this issue:

> But they [gay men] can also participate in a way in sport that is not so competitive, where the goal isn't like crushing your opponent . . . little scenes kind of capture it for me when I was in the New York

Gay Games. I visited a volleyball game and, you know, to see some really queeny-acting guys out there, you know, giving each other [high fives] with limp wrists—I thought it was fabulous, because they were out there playing, having a good time, but also not worried about presenting a macho image connected to sport. (interview, November 20, 1996)

The principles of inclusion, participation, and doing one's "personal" best enable Games participants to find a sport or cultural pursuit to engage with and find meaning in. Chess, bridge, and darts were added to the Amsterdam Games to enable the less athletic, as well as those living with illness, to participate. Sports at the Games are required by the Federation of Gay Games to cater to all levels of ability, from novice to advanced, and to be inclusive of people with disabilities. Many of the participants I interviewed remarked on the encouraging sport environment they found at the Games. For instance, competitors were cheered regardless of placing first or last in a swimming or running event, and no official Games records were kept as benchmarks of achievement.

However, as the Games have increased in size and stature, more elite performers and competitive motivations have come to the fore. This has in part been encouraged by the desire of Games organizers for recognition and publicity. The involvement of world champions and the breaking of international masters' sport records promote credibility. On the other hand, inclusiveness also extends to elite gay and lesbian athletes, who have enjoyed the affirming environment of the Gay Games as well.

Winston, an African American wrestler who attended the Vancouver and New York Games, recalls the increasingly competitive nature of the Games. Winning medals was very important to his team, which was from San Francisco:

There were several rivalries going on between wrestlers from San Francisco, New York, LA, [and] some from France and other places. We were the biggest contingent. Like we didn't really talk to anybody. Gene [the team coach] kept us separate from other people, you know, he was building the mystique. . . . Our people wanted to win medals and we liked the idea of keeping ourselves separate from the other wrestlers, but we were friendly with them but we didn't want to give away any secrets. (interview, November 24, 1996)

So as not to give away their wrestling moves, Winston's team practiced separately from other teams by renting a dedicated training space in Vancouver and New York. Coach Gene Dermody stated that the team received some criticism for isolating itself. This was viewed by others as going against the ethos of the Gay Games, where participation and friendship take central importance. Gene also expressed his conservative political affiliations and his firmly held belief that gay men should be given the same male bonding experiences as straight men. This contrasted with Terry's perspective on the "queening" of volleyball as well as the uniquely campy and queer Pink Flamingo event.

The Pink Flamingo is the only truly unique queer sporting event to come out of the Gay Games and was invented by gay swimmers in the best traditions of camp. It started out as a simple drag and synchronized swimming performance by swimmer Charlie Carson at a private party after the swimming competition at the first Gay Games (Sowers 1994:30–31). The Pink Flamingo developed into a major drag performance and relay involving the carrying of tacky pink flamingos as batons. It has become more elaborate each year and provides a wonderfully playful antidote to the serious and meticulously officiated swimming competitions of the Gay Games and the IGLA Championships.[10]

Gender and sexuality-bending playfulness, political commentary and satire, scripted pool deck theater, and moving performances commemorating AIDS (New York Games) have also marked the evolution of this queer sport event. At the Amsterdam Games, the London team upstaged all other teams with a poolside reenactment of street scenes of Amsterdam and London, and an ornate replica of the Royal Yacht *Britannia,* the latter taking Queen Elizabeth II across the swimming pool to meet Queen Beatrix of Amsterdam (John, interview, July 19, 2006). Lesbian swimmers have been somewhat marginalized by the exaggerated performances of and play on the conventionally heterosexy and "emphasized" femininity that exemplifies drag; however, they have participated in water ballet commemorating their male teammates who have died of AIDS. This marked the bringing together of lesbians and gay men around the political battles and shared communities of care concerned with AIDS. And there were also the well-remembered all-women's Pink Flamingo teams like the West Hollywood women, who wore men's bathing suits stuffed with paper towels to make phallic bulges. These women swam backstroke while topless, with black tape across their nipples and inflatable guitars (serving as relay batons) positioned between their legs (Sowers 1994:30–31).

Proactive efforts have been made to involve women more equally in the organization and programming of the Gay Games. All thirty-plus sports since the New York Games have been open to women, and there have been targeted promotional efforts to encourage women's participation at most of the Games. Women's outreach was especially pursued at the Amsterdam Games. Outreach involved quotas to increase women's registration as participants (43 percent of total), scholarships that subsidized economically disadvantaged women, preferential hosted housing for women, and the staging of a women's festival (van Leeuwen 1998). All Gay Games have had women's and men's cochairs for all leadership positions, and most have had a women's advisory committee to promote women's participation and perspectives within the Games.

Lindy McKnight had been involved with organizing the squash competition at the first two Gay Games, and she had played squash in the third. She valued the opportunities the Games presented to women, including the opportunity to compete in nontraditional sports such as power lifting, rugby, wrestling, and ice hockey without experiencing stigma. She elaborated further:

> There is really no other event which is so open and so encouraging of women to participate in sport. Even with the Olympics it is limited. But here is an opportunity for women to play sport and compete in sport and be rewarded in sport and be acknowledged in sport that I can't think of anywhere else it exists, particularly for older women. Now, because you have the Gay Games, you have city after city, organizing year round for all four years between the Games, racquetball leagues and ice hockey games. Because enough interest has been generated, women have networked, they have found each other, they have rented community centers, they have set up leagues, they have set up ways to stay sharp, to stay competitive, and they have a goal to work towards. It's got to have an incredible sociological impact on local communities . . . and all of a sudden these are global too and that's a huge opportunity and encouragement for women. (interview, November 18, 1996)

Roz had played baseball with the boys' team when she was nine years old, softball in high school, and then graduated to playing within a closeted lesbian league based in New York during her twenties. She found the Gay Games very affirming for lesbian athletes:

> [At the Games] it's okay to be a dyke. . . . I mean that, whenever you are a woman at any age, even a girl playing sports, there is always this undercurrent of "Are you a lesbian?" I went to a college who had a woman's basketball team that was the best in the country and it was known that the coach would not draft lesbians and would tell parents when recruiting that she doesn't allow lesbians on the team and if [she] found out she would kick you off the team—she kicked the number one player off the team one year. I think that [at the Games] you do not have to deal with this at all. There is no questioning, no wondering, you don't have to put on makeup to play, or worry how long your shorts are, how short your shorts are, how your bra is—you can be totally free. (interview, December 2, 1996)

Heather, coming from a more politically active, lesbian, feminist soccer team named Hackney, had a different perspective on the meaning of sport (interview, December 12, 1996). Hackney was the first "out" team to compete in London's local women's soccer league. The team also participated in the Gay Games IV. The team was organized on feminist collective principles, with the majority of team decisions made by consensus. The team's organizational structure was flat (i.e., not hierarchical), with few leadership positions, the latter mainly to satisfy the requirements of London's "mainstream" soccer league. Hackney's collectivist spirit of play emphasized the inclusion of all skill levels, an appreciation of achievements, a concentration on the process and pleasure of the game above outcomes, and comprehensive equal opportunity policies (Symons 2002:110).

There are lesbian feminist sport collectives in North America and Australia as well—for instance, the Parkville field hockey club in Melbourne, the Flying Bats soccer team (also informed by queer politics) in Sydney, the Notso Amazons softball league in Canada, as well as many lesbian softball teams the United States (Litchfield and Symons 2011; McDonald 2011; Birrell and Richter 1987).

Negative Experiences

While the responses of Gay Games participants have been overwhelmingly positive, negative experiences have been reported that diminished community feeling. Participants in the triathlon at the

New York Games expressed varying degrees of disappointment and frustration. The swimming leg of this event had to be canceled because of inadequate emergency medical aid (Labreque 1994:54–55). Cyclists and track and field athletes at the Amsterdam Games also faced organizational difficulties (K. Rowe, interview, February 16, 2003; C. Meade, interview, January 30, 2007). At the Chicago Games, organizers were ill prepared for a major heat wave and this impacted negatively on a number of sports events (Davis 2006). The competitiveness of the swimming events has also sometimes overwhelmed novice swimmers at the Games. This feeling of being overwhelmed was the strongest memory recalled by Kathryn, an Australian woman who'd had no competitive sport experience since attending secondary school (interview, December 13, 1998). The Amsterdam Gay Games was to be her great adventure. After twenty-six years of marriage and raising four children, she had come out as a lesbian and the Games beckoned as a premier queer community experience. Kathryn recalled negative experiences of sport and physical education at school and envisaged the Gay Games to be more inclusive. Unfortunately, this was not the case, as the swimming competition at the Amsterdam Games seemed to cater mainly to experienced swimmers, and the officiating was formalized and intimidating rather than friendly and encouraging.

Political friction and inequality based especially on gender and race were evident in the political debates that occurred behind the scenes during some of the Gay Games, and also in many of the central promotional images used to market and celebrate the Games, which centered on young, white, middle-class, muscular, fit, able-bodied, and attractive gay men. This affluent basis of Games attendance was succinctly encapsulated by an oppositional group at the Amsterdam Games in their slogan: "The Gay Games is 'The PAY Games'" (Symons 2010:162). Scholarships, hosted housing, and budget accommodations were practical strategies used during the Gay Games IV–VII to enable the less affluent to participate.

There have also been a variety of homophobic incidents experienced by Gay Games organizers and participants (Symons 2010:1–82, 55–58, 105–106, 176–177, 230–232). One of the sources of this opposition has been fundamentalist Christians. In the lead-up to the Vancouver Games, a group of unnamed "Christian leaders who live in Vancouver" launched a well-organized and virulent advertising campaign in the media against the event (Green 1988:6). The fundamentalist discourse portrayed gays as "sex-crazed, sick, disease-ridden 'animals'—a public health menace and abomination to god-fearing Christian society" (Symons 2010:81). Games organizers astutely lobbied newspapers, civil rights organizations, and politicians to support the event, and the public response, as expressed in the media, was overwhelmingly opposed to the fundamentalist perspective. A coalition of gay and lesbian community members and heterosexual allies was formed in the face of this homophobia. The director of the Vancouver Games, Shawn Kelly, observed that "to a large extent these particular ads backfired and one of the main immediate responses had been a tremendous outpouring of offers to volunteer, and financial support was given" (quoted in MVA&AA 1990). This experience of being so virulently "othered" forged stronger community-making. Christian fundamentalist opposition was also experienced during other Games. I recall being confronted by placard-waving demonstrators with the message "God made Adam and Eve not Adam and Steve" as I walked into the grounds of the Ajax Stadium for the opening ceremony of the Amsterdam Games. A larger and more vocal group of demonstrators confronted Chicago Games participants during the closing ceremony with messages of sin, hell, and redemption for homosexuality. The majority of Games participants appeared to take these experiences in stride, but some may have found them unsettling. These experiences certainly contrasted with the joy, affirmation, and community celebration of the Games ceremonies.

Conclusion

All of the eight Gay Games that have been held since 1982 have sought to include a multiplicity of individuals, teams, and communities. The international LGBT community that attends these Games is also diverse, although the majority are from the affluent, developed nations of the world. There is no universal sense of gay and lesbian identity, as LGBT identities, behaviors, and ways of life are not universal across cultures, and specific programs that enable LGBT people from less developed countries to attend the Gay Games have to be sensitive to the cultural specifics of a variety of sex/gender systems within the world. Differences such as gender, race, ethnicity, socioeconomic class, ability, and politics among the broad community who engage in the Gay Games can also impede the imagining of a common social space.

The "webs of significance" that sustain communities, such as shared meanings, solidarity, belonging, participation, and inclusion, have been fostered at the Gay Games. This has been achieved through the very public celebration of people who are often rendered invisible and "othered." Affirmation is most strongly experienced when Gay Games participants visibly occupy important public places, and during Games ceremonies "where their common cultures are celebrated and common concerns are recognised" (Symons 2002:111). By marching in the televised public arena of the opening ceremonies as well as competing in the sports events and performing in the cultural programs, Games participants "come in" to this diverse and affirming community as well as "come out" as LGBT. Pride, identity, and community-making are explicit social outcomes of the Gay Games. An extensive network of sport, recreational, and cultural clubs, associations, and leagues have grown from or have been augmented by the Gay Games, providing ongoing social connections of friendship, support, and reciprocity as well as opportunities to learn, develop, and enjoy new skills, abilities, and activities, all of which promote individual and community development.

The Gay Games are remarkably inclusive in policy and practice, as exemplified by power-sharing among women and men and specific strategies to promote the participation of people from less advantaged and less representative groups, including women, people with disabilities, transgender individuals, ethnic/racial minorities, people from developing countries, and people having low socioeconomic status. This inclusive culture is also integral to sport competition. There are no qualifying standards, official medal tallies, or Games records, and both the novice and the elite performer are usually catered to at the Games. Self-esteem and community esteem are productively experienced during the Gay Games: "health, vigour, talent, joy, working and playing together, respecting difference, striving for inclusiveness, as well as organisational, commercial, cultural and sporting achievement, are some of the ideal reflections circulated in the gay and mainstream media and retold as stories of significance by many participants and organizers" (Symons 2002:111).

There have also been stories of organizational mismanagement, financial crisis, and major divisions within the international gay sport movement. These are also part of community-making. All diverse communities experience differences of perspective and conflict as well as inequalities of power and representation, and the LGBT community of the Gay Games is no exception.

Notes

1. The brief details on the first World Outgames were informed by three interviews with organizers of that event.

2. See Symons 2010:1–12 for more details on the method used and a complete list of interviews.

3. Also see Carlson 1982 for the main gay news reporting of the first Gay Games and its opening ceremony.

4. See chapter 9 of Symons 2010 for a more in-depth exploration of transgender participation at the Gay Games and especially at the Sydney Games of 2002.

5. There were 12,099 participants in total, from 77 countries; 43 percent were from the United States and 25 percent were from Europe, with women comprising 31 percent of overall participants. See Symons 2010:250–256.

6. There were deficits for Gay Games III–VI, with the deficit in Sydney in 2002 being the most substantial. See Symons 2010:250–251 for further details.

7. The first North American Outgames were held in Calgary in 2007. The European Gay and Lesbian Sports Federation, founded in 1989, governs the annual Eurogames. First staged in The Hague in 1992, this multisport and human rights event is one the largest LGBT events to be held annually in Europe, attracting up to 5,000 participants each year. See http://www.eurogames.info/eurogames-history.html.

8. Gay Games VIII (2010) attracted 10,000 participants, and the second World Outgames (2009) attracted 8,000 participants.

9. People from Western nations who are currently living with HIV and AIDS do so for long periods of time (due to effective medication and health practices), and while the impact of AIDS is still significant, it is not as dramatic and devastating on the LGBT community as it was during the height of the epidemic in the 1980s and early 1990s.

10. Terry Allison and I are currently researching the history of the Pink Flamingo and have interviewed over thirty-five participants.

7

Reducing Sexual Prejudice

George B. Cunningham

In his children's book *The Crayon Box that Talked,* Shane DeRolf relays the story of a girl who purchases a box of talking crayons. While that occurrence is remarkable enough, the story continues to relay how the crayons bicker with one another, each voicing dissatisfaction with the other. Upon hearing this, the girl decides to lay out all of the crayons on her bed so they can watch her draw a picture. With this they come to appreciate how they can collectively make something new (e.g., yellow and blue make green) and how each color uniquely contributes to the overall picture. The story concludes with all the crayons observing, "We are a box of crayons, each one of us unique. But when we get together . . . the picture is complete" (1997:21–22).

In addition to being one of my daughters' favorite books, I find that *The Crayon Box that Talked* is also relevant to the discussion of reducing sexual prejudice. Just as the crayons' antagonism toward one another was reduced when they saw how each color was needed to create the picture, I argue in this chapter that people's sexual prejudice is likely to be reduced when they recognize the contributions of people who have varied sexual and gender identities. In doing so, I draw from various theories in social psychology, applied psychology, and geography to develop an integrated framework (see Figure 7.1) based on social categorization as a foundation.

Figure 7.1 Influence of Intergroup Contact and Diversity Culture on Diversity Mind-Sets and Sexual Prejudice

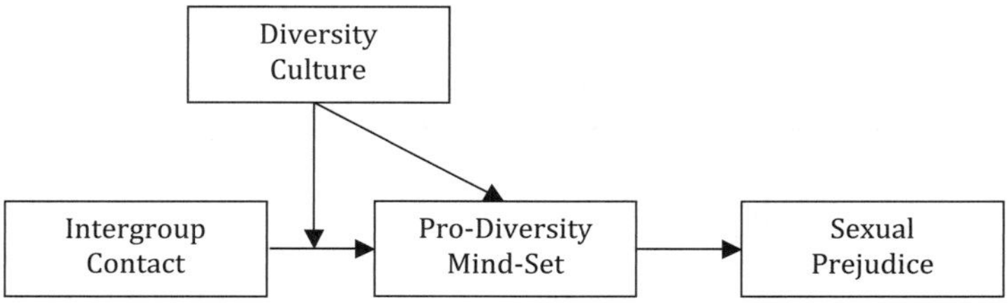

Theoretical Framework: Social Categorization

The social categorization framework, which collectively draws from self-categorization theory (Turner et al. 1987) and social identity theory (Tajfel and Turner 1979), holds that, as a way of making sense of a complex social world, people classify themselves and others into groups. This can be done based on a myriad of characteristics, such as demographic characteristics, religious beliefs, or even the sport teams that one follows. Thus, people come to define themselves and others in terms of their social identity (Tajfel and Turner 1979). They then use these identities to differentiate in-group members, or others who are similar to the self, from out-group members, or persons who differ from the self. These group distinctions are likely to be magnified when the group membership is important to the individual (e.g., being a bisexual is an important part of one's identity), when the particular diversity dimension is salient within that context (e.g., issues surrounding sexual orientation are prevalent in the workplace), or a combination of the two. In general, people will view in-group members more favorably than they will out-group members, resulting in subsequent differences in a host of outcomes, such as liking, trust, support, and helping behaviors, among others. Thus there exists the potential for intergroup bias and the subsequent stereotyping, prejudice, and discrimination that can occur.

The social categorization process is fundamental to a discussion of sexual prejudice and strategies to reduce it. Specifically, people are likely to view persons who have a sexual orientation that is similar to their own, or whom they perceive to have a similar sexual orientation (see Sartore and Cunningham 2009b), more favorably than they are those individuals who have a sexual orientation that is different from their own. As a result, people whose sexual orientation differs from that of the typical majority are likely to face prejudice and discrimination. In fact, Anne Tsui, Terri Egan, and Charles O'Reilly (1992) suggested that the formation of in-groups and out-groups was fundamental to employees' preferences to work with similar others.

The extant literature provides support for the negative effects of being a member of a sexual orientation out-group. For example, researchers have shown that lesbian coaches sometimes face hostility from heterosexual administrators (Krane and Barber 2005), that sexual minorities experience anxiety and dread when contemplating whether to disclose their sexual orientation to their heterosexual coworkers (Ragins, Singh, and Cornwell 2007), that people who are lesbian, gay, or bisexual (LGB) face discrimination in the hiring and selection process (Cunningham, Sartore, and McCullough 2010; Hebl et al. 2002), and that women working in health and kinesiology departments are often presumed to be gay and therefore face prejudices and negative treatment similar to that faced by LGB faculty (Sartore and Cunningham 2010).

Diversity Mind-Sets

If social categorization and intergroup bias are fundamental to understanding sexual prejudice, then what steps can be taken to reduce such bias? While several options remain (for a review, see Pettigrew 1998), I argue here that perhaps the most effective is to focus on the value of diversity. Specifically, when leaders and organizational cultures emphasize the manner in which diversity positively contributes to desired processes and outcomes, then people's differences will come to be seen as an asset, not a detriment. In this way, people appreciate that dissimilar others can uniquely contribute to their own understanding and learning, be a source of enrichment, and positively contribute to the team or organization. As a result, their attitude toward dissimilar others is improved, not in spite of, but *because of* the nature of the differences.

Two theoretical positions support these arguments. The first is Miles Hewstone and Rupert Brown's (1986) mutual group differentiation model, which suggests that intergroup bias is reduced when in-group and out-group members come to see the superiorities and weaknesses associated with both groups. In doing so, they come to see how contributions from both groups are needed to reach the desired end. The second is Daan van Knippenberg and colleagues' work related to diversity mind-sets (van Knippenberg and Haslam 2003; van Knippenberg and Schippers 2007), which suggests that diversity can positively influence group processes and outcomes when group members hold pro-diversity beliefs. As van Knippenberg and M. Schippers note, diversity's effects "should be more positive in contexts where individuals, groups, and organizations have more favorable beliefs about and attitudes toward diversity, are more focused on harvesting the benefits of diversity, and have a better understanding of how to realize these benefits" (2007:531).

Though empirical examination of these tenets is somewhat limited, there is support for these contentions. Robin Ely and David Thomas's (2001) qualitative investigation represents one of the earlier and more cited examples. The authors interviewed seventy-eight employees from three culturally diverse firms. They also conducted participant observation and content analysis of various organizational materials. Ely and Thomas found that in one organizational culture (integration and learning), diversity was considered to inform and improve work processes and outcomes. Within this context, employees saw diversity as a source of learning and renewal; managers integrated diversity and inclusion principles throughout the organizational system; and a diverse set of employees held leadership and decision-making positions. Not surprisingly, employees in this type of organization felt valued and respected by their coworkers and supervisors, and they reported a general sense of well-being. The authors did not observe these dynamics in the other workplaces they investigated.

More recent studies also point to the value of having positive diversity beliefs. In one example, van Knippenberg, S. Alexander Haslam, and Michael Platow (2007) conducted two studies, the first a cross-sectional examination of 220 Dutch employees and the second an experimental study of 126 Dutch undergraduate students. In both studies, they examined how the relationship between a group's gender diversity and identification with the group would be moderated by the individual's diversity beliefs. Results from both studies supported the notion that when people have positive attitudes toward gender diversity, they are more likely to strongly identify with diverse groups.

These results are congruent with those observed by Astrid Homan and colleagues (2007). In this experimental study, the authors found that informationally diverse groups performed better when the group members believed that diversity improved group functioning. Diversity beliefs did not influence how well homogeneous groups performed. The authors also found that elaboration of task-relevant information mediated this relationship. Thus, when diverse groups believe that diversity benefits the group, they are likely to share more information with one another, which in turn is likely to improve performance. These findings are wholly consistent with the categorization-elaboration model (van Knippenberg, De Dreu, and Homan 2004), which holds that, given the right conditions (e.g., when pro-diversity beliefs are high), group differences are likely to be a source of enrichment, understanding, and effectiveness.

Finally, I too have observed the benefits of pro-diversity beliefs, in a study of 157 college students participating in racially diverse physical activity classes (Cunningham 2010a). Three findings are particularly germane to the current discussion. First, pro-diversity beliefs were associated with greater satisfaction with other students in the class. Second, race moderated these effects, such that the relationship between pro-diversity beliefs and satisfaction with classmates was stronger for whites than for racial minorities. This suggests that when whites felt that diversity benefited the class, they expressed more positive attitudes toward all students, those both racially similar and racially dissimilar to the self. Finally, both pro-diversity beliefs and satisfaction with classmates were associated with positive evaluations of the class itself.

Benefits of Sexual Orientation Diversity

As the preceding review makes clear, pro-diversity beliefs can transform people's attitudes toward out-group members and diverse groups as a whole, and, as a result, can serve as the basis for reducing sexual prejudice. This conversation is based on the idea that the individual differences can be beneficial. But is there evidence that sexual orientation diversity—something sport managers seemingly try to minimize—can be beneficial? The extant literature suggests that this is indeed the case.

E. Nicole Melton and I (Cunningham and Melton 2011) have developed a theoretical framework to articulate the benefits of sexual orientation diversity to sport organizations. We first argue that sexual orientation diversity allows for enhanced decisionmaking capabilities. This position is consistent with van Knippenberg and colleagues' (2004) categorization-elaboration model, which holds that diverse groups consist of people from different backgrounds, with varied experiences, and unique ways of approaching tasks. These characteristics result in a broader depth of understanding and greater decisionmaking comprehensiveness, both of which should improve overall performance. And there is research to support the notion that LGB individuals have unique experiences and perspectives, relative to their heterosexual counterparts. For instance, the sexual prejudice they experience throughout their lives (Herek 2009; Meyer 2003) can help to develop crisis competence (Friend 1991) and an ability to critically analyze prevailing social structures and ways of knowing (Anderson 2000; Pastrana 2006). Furthermore, sexual minorities sometimes display distinctive leadership styles that emphasize creativity and inclusiveness (Snyder 2006), both of which are associated with performance gains. Finally, LGB employees are more likely to travel than are heterosexuals. This is important because travel, particularly when abroad, is associated with improved cross-cultural skills, global competence, empathy for others, and inclusive attitudes toward dissimilar others (Kitsantas 2004; Lindsey 2005). All of these points suggest that LGB individuals provide unique perspectives and attributes to the group—characteristics that should improve the group's decisionmaking capabilities.

Second, we theorize that sexual orientation diversity can result in improved marketplace understanding (Cunningham and Melton 2011). LGB persons represent between 4 and 17 percent of the US population (Lubensky et al. 2004), and through their spending, estimated to be about $600 billion annually (Day and Greene 2008), they also make a meaningful economic impact. These figures suggest that sexual minorities represent a sizable and potentially lucrative target market. Sexual orientation diversity allows organizations to effectively tap into this target market because it increases the ability to understand the needs, wants, and desires of LGB consumers. There is both conceptual support (Robinson and Dechant 1997) and empirical support (Cunningham 2008a; Cunningham and Singer 2009) for the connection between organizational diversity and the ability to capture a diverse target market.

Third, we argue that sexual orientation diversity will generate goodwill among consumers (Cunningham and Melton 2011). This position is based on the notion that there is a "moral obligation for organizations to be accepting of all employees, irrespective of their individual differences" (Cunningham and Fink 2006:455). And if this moral obligation exists, then external stakeholders should be keenly aware of whether the organization fulfills this duty, and subsequently reward or penalize that entity accordingly. While only recently emerging, there is some evidence that stakeholder groups do just that. Melton (2010a) conducted an experiment with job applicants and found that they were more attracted to LGB-inclusive organizations than they were to workplaces that were not. Harris Interactive polls (see HarrisInteractive.com) found that sexual minorities are particularly aware of how LGB-friendly an organization is, and their loyalty and consumptive behaviors follow accordingly. Finally, in an examination in the sport context, we also observed that sexual minorities express greater loyalty to sport organizations they perceive to be LGB-friendly compared to other sport organizations (Melton, Cunningham, and McCullough 2010).

Our position related to goodwill suggests that external stakeholders (e.g., consumers, job applicants) are aware of and base their decisions upon how inclusive an organization is. Richard Florida's (2003, 2004) creative capital theory extends this argument further. He suggests that creative people drive regional economic activity and that they are attracted to areas where there is a large concentration of innovation and technological advancements (i.e., technology), where the populace is highly educated (i.e., talent), and where the culture is one of diversity and inclusion (i.e., tolerance). The last point is of particular interest here. Florida convincingly argues that locales with a high concentration of sexual minorities are likely to be most tolerant of others. After all, Americans have more negative attitudes toward LGB individuals than they do toward other marginalized groups (Herek 2009; see also Gill et al. 2006), and in many ways, sexual prejudice is still socially acceptable. For evidence of the latter point, consider that employment discrimination against LGB individuals is legal in the majority of US states. Accordingly, Florida suggested that if a region is LGB-inclusive, then it is likely inclusive of all persons. Specifically, he noted: "As a group, gays have been subject to a particularly high level of discrimination. Attempts by gays to integrate into the mainstream of society have met substantial opposition. To some extent, homosexuality represents the last frontier of diversity in our society, and thus a place that welcomes the gay community welcomes all kinds of people" (Florida 2003:13). His qualitative and quantitative data (2002, 2003, 2004) lend considerable support to these arguments.

Florida's creative capital theory, while set within the context of regional economic development, is also applicable to sport organizations. That is, creative individuals are likely to be attracted to workplaces where technology is advanced, other talented people are employed, and a culture of diversity and inclusiveness exists. Furthermore, LGB-inclusiveness, because it is so scarce in many sport organizations (see Cunningham 2010c), should be one of the strongest signals of an inclusive work environment. S. Douglas Pugh and colleagues made similar arguments, suggesting that employee diversity can serve as an *"extracted cue* in which people develop a larger sense of what is occurring" (2008:1424, emphasis original).

In a test of this relationship, I collected data from senior-level athletic administrators from 199 National Collegiate Athletic Association (NCAA) Division III athletic departments (Cunningham 2011a). In addition to gathering information about the sexual orientation and the collective commitment to diversity within the department, I also assessed the degree to which the opportunity provided opportunities to be creative. After controlling for other diversity measures and the size of the department, results indicate that sexual orientation diversity interacted with commitment to diversity to predict the presence of a creative work environment. Creative potential was highest when both sexual orientation diversity and commitment to diversity were high. These findings show that Florida's (2003, 2004) theory is applicable in the organizational setting, and that, in addition to sexual orientation diversity, it is important to have a work environment supportive of employee differences.

Finally, while there is strong theoretical evidence of the benefits of sexual orientation diversity (Cunningham and Melton 2011; Day and Greene 2008; Florida 2002, 2003) and some empirical evidence linking sexual orientation diversity with key mediating mechanisms, such as a creative work environment (Cunningham 2011a), examination of sexual orientation diversity's impact on objective measures of performance is largely lacking. This is an important consideration, because, as Janet Fink and Donna Pastore note, "while it would be wonderful for all of those in positions of power to realize the moral and social advantages of diversity, it may not be a realistic goal. Thus, for diversity initiatives to be truly embedded within the organization, those in power must be convinced of diversity's relationship to organizational effectiveness" (1999:314).

With this in mind, I conducted a study (Cunningham 2011b) to examine the association between sexual orientation diversity and organizational performance among 239 NCAA Division I athletic departments. Data included information about the department's sexual orientation diversity and its culture of diversity in general, and an objective measure of performance—the National Association of Collegiate Directors of Athletics (NACDA) Director's Cup points. This is an award given on an annual basis to the top athletic department, with points earned based on the women's and men's team performances, and it is generally recognized as an objective assessment of "the best overall athletic department" (Timanus 2010). After controlling for other diversity variables and the size of the athletic department, results indicate that sexual orientation diversity and diversity culture interacted to predict departmental performance. As expected, performance was highest when both variables were high. Of particular note, departments with high sexual orientation diversity and very inclusive cultures had nearly seven times more NACDA points than departments with low sexual orientation diversity and an inclusive work culture (see Figure 7.2).

Thus the evidence is clear: LGB employees positively contribute to workplace effectiveness. The theoretical and empirical evidence

Figure 7.2 Relationship Among Sexual Orientation Diversity, Culture, and Organizational Performance

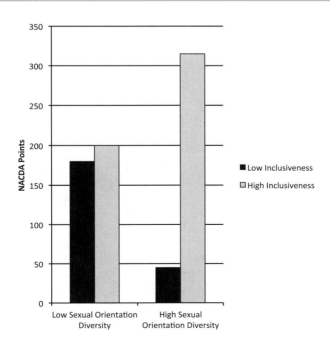

unequivocally shows that sexual orientation diversity (i.e., an increase in the presence of sexual minorities) results in better decision-making, improved marketplace understanding, enhanced goodwill, attraction of a talented work force, a more creative work environment, and other objective measures of success. As such, managers seeking to reduce sexual prejudice by demonstrating the benefits of sexual orientation diversity (i.e., influencing people's diversity mind-sets) have compelling support for their contentions.

Influencing Diversity Mind-Sets

Thus far I have discussed how people with pro-diversity mind-sets have positive attitudes toward heterogeneous groups and toward people who are dissimilar to the self, and I have highlighted the various ways in which sexual orientation diversity benefits sport organizations. I now turn to an analysis of how sport managers can convey this information to influence people's diversity mind-sets. Several options are viable, such as intergroup contact and establishing a culture of diversity and inclusion, the latter of which includes leader support, diversity training, and systemic integration.

Intergroup Contact

According to Brown and Hewstone's (2005) intergroup contact theory, contact between in-group and out-group members should reduce intergroup bias, particularly when the out-group member is prototypical. Contact allows people to learn about one another, thereby serving to dispel myths and stereotypes about out-group members, represents a behavioral change, reduces intergroup anxieties, and has the potential to result in a reappraisal of the out-group (Allport 1954). In the context of the current discussion, contact between LGB individuals and heterosexuals should allow both parties to observe commonalities with one another, break down assumptions about homogeneity of the other groups, and realize that their backgrounds and perspectives can be a source of richness and understanding. Typicality is important, because it allows the bias reduction to be transferred to other out-group members. If intergroup relationships occur with someone who is not believed to be a prototypical member of the out-group, then the positives can be chalked up as an anomaly (e.g., "I can learn a lot from Rosie, but she is not a typical lesbian"). However, when typicality is high, then the positive attitudes directed toward the individual have the potential to transfer to other members of that social group.

Jens Binder and colleagues' (2009) longitudinal study of high school–aged youth provides one of the most comprehensive analyses of this perspective. They collected field surveys from 1,665 students in Germany, Belgium, and England, asking them about their intergroup friendships, intergroup anxiety, and prejudice. As the authors expected, both the amount and the quality of the contact that students had with out-group members were predictive of the prejudice they felt six months later. The authors also observed that these effects were moderated by the typicality of the out-group member: contact was more strongly related to prejudice reduction when typicality was high than when it was low.

Culture of Diversity and Inclusion

While there is compelling evidence for the benefits of intergroup contact, recent research with sexual minorities suggests that contact alone might not be sufficient. Rather, in line with Gordon Allport's (1954) ideas related to optimal conditions of contact, this research suggests that the benefits of sexual orientation diversity are best realized when there is a strong commitment to diversity (Cunningham 2011a) or within an organizational culture of diversity and inclusion (Cunningham 2011b). Thus, sport organizations must have the needed structure and organizational culture in place to effectively convey and realize the benefits of sexual orientation diversity. This includes, among other things, support from top leaders, offering diversity training, and systemically integrating inclusion principles throughout the workplace.

Top managers, whether chief executive officers, coaches, or team captains, play a key role in shaping the diversity culture of the workplace and in enhancing employees' pro-diversity attitudes. Their steadfast support for diversity and inclusion serves as a model for others to emulate. Albert Bandura's social cognitive theory points to these effects, as he noted that "virtually all learning phenomena, resulting from direct experience, can occur vicariously by observing other people's behaviors and the consequences for them" (1986:19). Thus, when sport managers advocate sexual minorities' inclusion in the workplace, actively combat heterosexism, and champion the benefits that sexual orientation diversity brings to the workplace, other managers and employees are also likely to follow suit. Researchers have offered empirical support for this, too. Jacqueline Gilbert and J. Ivancevich (2000) observed that strong CEO support for diversity efforts served as a catalyst for similar enthusiasm expressed throughout the organization. In my qualitative research with John Singer (Cunningham and Singer 2009), participants suggested that athletic directors modeled the diversity-related attitudes and behaviors expected from others within the department. Not only did these athletic directors vocally champion inclusion, but they also participated in diversity-related activities, such as training, alongside other departmental members.

A culture of diversity and inclusion is also enhanced through diversity training, or the "formal efforts to enable development of awareness, knowledge, and skills to effectively work with, work for, and manage diverse others in various contexts" (Bell, Connerley, and Cocchiara 2009:598). Diverse and inclusive sport organizations routinely make use of these educational efforts (Cunningham and Singer 2009). And while these efforts do not always have the intended benefits (Kalev, Dobbin, and Kelly 2006), there is evidence that diversity training programs provide a number of advantages, including more positive attitudes toward diversity, a greater understanding of dissimilar others, and more inclusive behaviors among employees (for a review, see Kulik and Roberson 2008). Within the context of the current discussion, diversity training could be used to inform employees and team players of the many benefits associated with sexual orientation diversity, thereby shaping their pro-diversity beliefs. Indeed, researchers have shown that simply providing people with information about diversity and diversity initiatives can shape their subsequent attitudes and behaviors (Cunningham and Fitzgerald 2006; van Knippenberg, Haslam, and Platow 2007).

Finally, a culture of diversity and inclusion is best realized when managers systemically integrate diversity and inclusion principles (Cunningham 2008b; Cunningham and Singer 2009). This means ensuring that organizational values, the mission statement, strategic goals, personnel decisions, marketing efforts, and the like, are all consistent with principles of diversity and inclusion. In this way, diversity impacts the entire organization and contributes to its success. This stands in contrast to efforts among some sport managers and coaches to emphasize diversity in some areas but not in others (for an example, see Cunningham 2009). Not only does the latter approach reduce diversity's potency, but it also opens the door for activities in some organizational subunits to seemingly contradict one another—something that can result in external stakeholders interpreting mixed signals about the organization's commitment to diversity. In fact, when diversity and inclusion initiatives are not systemically integrated, the programs that are in place are likely to fail or have limited effectiveness (Agars and Kottke 2004; Cunningham 2009).

Conclusion

I began this chapter with a discussion of DeRolf's magical crayons, who came to like one another only after realizing their potential synergistic effects and the manner in which each crayon uniquely contributed to the beauty of the picture. At the risk of oversimplifying the issue, I drew from this story to make parallel arguments related to sexual orientation in sport organizations. Sexual prejudice is likely to be reduced when people come to see that sexual orientation diversity positively contributes to the workplace. Indeed, an increase of sexual minorities in the workplace is associated with a bevy of benefits: decisionmaking comprehensiveness, marketplace understanding, goodwill among external stakeholders, attraction of talented employees, a creative work environment, and other objective measures of success. Further, sport managers can take several steps to ensure that employees are aware of these benefits, including providing strong support for LGB individuals and creating and sustaining an organizational culture of diversity and inclusion. In short, when sport organization employees realize the benefits of sexual orientation diversity and come to see differences as a source of learning, enrichment, and competitive advantage, not only will sexual prejudice be reduced, but the entire workplace will be characterized by diversity, openness, and inclusion.

8

What's Next?

Melanie L. Sartore-Baldwin

When most think of sport, they think of boys/men and girls/ women engaging in some kind of physical competition that ultimately results in a winner and a loser—nothing more, nothing less. Ideally, the realm of sport would be so simple, but as this book has shown, it is not. Sport is structured around strict ideological beliefs systems that have historically dictated who participates, coaches, manages, and spectates, and that have sanctioned the subsequent experiences of those granted access. To a large extent, these ideologically based sanctions still exist today, as those possessing the most power, status, and control are prototypically white, able-bodied, heterosexual men (Fink, Pastore, and Riemer 2001). Accordingly, issues of fairness surrounding race, ability, sexuality, and gender in sport continue to exist. With a specific focus on gender and sexual orientation, this book has provided a comprehensive look at sexual stigma and prejudice in sport.

In Chapter 1, the realm of sport was identified as a heterosexist institution that has long been utilized to reinforce traditional gender roles for men and women by privileging heterosexual masculinity over all other forms (Connell 1987, 1995; Messner 2002). Indeed, it is well established that gender is an institution whereby boys and men are to be big, strong, tough, and sexually attracted to women, while women are to be demure, physically weaker than men, attractive, and sexually attracted to men (Connell 1995). These arrangements have perhaps been most deeply ingrained in the realm of sport

129

(e.g., Azzarito and Solomon 2005; Schmalz and Kerstetter 2006). Accordingly, I presented a discussion of gender, sexual orientation, sexual stigma, and sexual prejudice within the sport context as the foundation for discussion of specific issues in subsequent chapters.

As Gregory Herek (2007, 2009) has noted, sexual stigma and prejudice are sociological and psychological phenomena that manifest structurally and individually, respectively. Thus, confronting sexual stigma and prejudice is no small undertaking, as sexual orientation and sexuality are linked to cultural debates, societal institutions, value systems, stereotypical beliefs, and strong emotions. The chapters in this book have sought to confront sexual stigma and prejudice within sport by discussing the topic from several vantage points. In Chapter 2, focusing on women, E. Nicole Melton drew from previous works and presented a multilevel model that identified antecedents, consequences, and outcomes of one of the most pervasive stigmas in sport—the lesbian stigma (e.g., Sartore and Cunningham 2009b, 2010). In doing so, Melton also identified several positive signs of changing attitudes toward nonheterosexual women in sport. In Chapter 3, focusing on men, Eric Anderson, Mark McCormack, and Matt Ripley also identified positive change by discussing the growing acceptance of homosexuality in sport, the increasing number of "out" athletes, and the evolution of homosexually themed language. Indicating a change in the culture, Anderson and colleagues believe that the realm of sport may no longer be as fraught with sexual prejudice and homophobia as it once was. Thus they conveyed, with great optimism, that inclusiveness will continue to improve on sport teams.

In Chapter 4, operating from a different vantage point, Erin Buzuvis discussed the nexus of gender, sport, and policy, specifically gender and sexual stigma in relation to the biological and physical characteristics assigned to men and women. Highlighting the fluidity of gender and sex and identifying individual's rights to self-define as an emerging consideration in the sport context, Buzuvis provided examples of the unique challenges that intersex, transsexual, and transgender athletes face. Among these challenges, however, Buzuvis identified several advances and successes that have been made in recent years. In Chapter 5, Nefertiti Walker also discussed a population who experience unique challenges—African American sexual minorities. Across sport (e.g., athletes, coaches, administrators), gay, lesbian, bisexual, and transsexual African Americans find themselves in a multiple-minority position whereby they may suffer profound levels of marginalization. E. Nicole Melton and George Cunningham's (2012) recent study of nonheterosexual women of different racial and ethnic backgrounds supports this notion.

In a visionary response to the prejudices experienced by sexual minorities in sport, Tom Waddell founded the Gay Games, as Caroline Symons explored in Chapter 6. Symons provided a detailed historical account of these Games and discussed the effects of them on the gay, lesbian, bisexual, and transsexual community. This history reveals that the shared connections between sexual minorities within an environment that values diversity and unity can empower nonheterosexual participants. Indeed, the guiding principles of "inclusion, participation, and personal best" established and maintained by the Federation of Gay Games should be embraced by every sport organization. This is not the case, however, as most sport organizations are fraught with inequalities despite the contributions of diverse work forces (e.g., Cunningham 2011a, 2011b). Recognizing this, George Cunningham offered an integrated framework in Chapter 7 highlighting the processes necessary for sport organizations to benefit from and provide a benefit to sexual minority employees.

While the study of sexual minorities in sport is relatively young, the presence of lesbian, gay, bisexual, transgender, and transsexual persons in the sport context is not. As Pat Griffin has noted, the increased visibility of sexual minorities in sport has allowed for their inclusion in discussions of equality and fairness (Sartore-Baldwin 2012). According to Anderson (2011a), this increased visibility is indicative of cultural shifts that have improved conditions for sexual minorities in sport. While the chapters in this book also suggest improved conditions, they elucidate the necessity for continued work as well. Indeed, with increased visibility comes increased scrutiny, challenges, and, in time, successes.

Where Do We Go from Here?

There are several examples of progress being made at nearly every level for sexual minorities in sport. Athletes at all levels (e.g., high school, college, professional) are "coming out" and subsequently receiving support from their teammates after doing so; sport programs and sport organizations are taking proactive measures to ensure that sexual minorities receive fair treatment and equal opportunities; and national and international governing bodies are reexamining, and in some instances reformulating, their policies and procedures of inclusion. Despite these advances, there is still a great deal of work to be done.

There is an ongoing need to study the motivations and manifestations of sexual prejudice and stigma and, correspondingly, a necessity to educate and provide resources about the antecedents and consequences of negativity toward sexual minorities. Herek's (2000) work has identified that sexual prejudice—the internalization of the stigmatization of sexual minorities (see Herek 2009)—is predicated on four primary underlying motivations, the first of which is experience, or lack thereof, with sexual minorities. A second motivation is a general fear of homosexuality as it relates to one's own sexual identity. Third, sexual prejudice is motivated by the need to maintain heterosexist social structures. Finally, perceiving incongruence between established societal group norms and the norms and values held by sexual minorities may also elicit sexual prejudice. Indeed, these motivations have consistently been found to correlate with and predict sexual prejudice among heterosexuals (e.g., Herek 1988, 2002; Norton and Herek (2012). To date, however, sexual prejudice has primarily been applied as a blanket concept to the sport context. Further examination of correlates and predictors such as lower levels of education, political conservatism, religious fundamentalism, psychological authoritarianism, and so on, should be integrated into the sport-related literature, as should the constructs of race, ethnicity, and the like. As Herek (2000) noted, research exploring the predictors of and constructs surround sexual prejudice can aid in successfully combating it.

Because the experiences of no two individuals are the same and attitudes toward different social groups differ, there is a need to dissect the sexual minority group and examine attitudes toward and experiences of gays, lesbians, bisexuals, transgender individuals, and transsexuals as unique entities (Worthen forthcoming). In sport, this is particularly the case for bisexuals, transgender people, and transsexuals, as there is a dearth of literature examining their experiences separate from those of gays and lesbians. In general, the predictors of heterosexuals' negative attitudes toward bisexuals and transgender persons are similar to the predictors of heterosexuals' negative attitudes toward gays and lesbians, but in the former case the negative attitudes themselves are stronger, particularly among men (Herek 2002; Norton and Herek 2012). These findings could have profound implications to the sport context where the gender binary remains strongly enforced, particularly for transgender persons. Not only do transgender identities blur gender lines, but also, in sport, transgender individuals have the potential to destabilize historically established structures. Given this, research should focus not only on inclusion of transgender individuals, but also on their unique experiences and protection against discrimination.

The importance of allies, advocacy, and education cannot be overstated. There are a number of programs that offer resources on the topics of sexuality, sexual orientation, and gender in the sport context (e.g., It Takes a Team; Changing the Game: The Gay, Lesbian, and Straight Education Network [GLSEN] Sports Project), as well as several speakers who offer workshops. As Pat Griffin points out, however, the use of these programs has not been consistent, nor has there been enough research on their effectiveness (Sartore-Baldwin 2012). Several outspoken sexual minorities have also offered their own personal experiences as teaching tools and sources of encouragement (e.g., Wade Davis, John Amaechi, Cyd Zeigler). Likewise, there have been heterosexuals who have spoken out against sexual prejudice (e.g., University of Massachusetts wrestler Hudson Taylor). Interestingly, most of these outspoken individuals are men, a surprising occurrence when considering the consistent finding that men hold more negative attitudes toward gays and lesbians than do women (e.g., Gill et al. 2006; Sartore and Cunningham 2009a).

Perhaps as a result of the pervasive lesbian stigma, women in sport may view advocating for sexual minority rights as a threat (Sartore and Cunningham 2009b). Self-stigma may also play a role, as sexual minorities must "scrutinize and change a myriad of longstanding attitudes, beliefs, emotions, and behavioral patterns in the course of coming out and overcoming self-stigma" (Herek 2007:913). Perhaps, too, the role of female advocates is more proximal to the sport setting, as research has found that openly lesbian athletes often credit a mentor or "trailblazer" with "paving the way" and making the coming-out process less fearful (Fink et al. 2012:91). Clearly, more research is needed to better determine how allies and advocates, of every sexual orientation, can help sexual minorities in sport.

There remains an undeniable sexual stigma within the sport context. It is present within youth and adolescent sport, intercollegiate sport, and professional sport, as well as among parents, participants, athletes, spectators, coaches, teachers, and many others. Though this stigma is being increasingly contested, more work is needed, as the heterosexist structures and individual attitudes toward sexual minorities in sport are deeply ingrained.

References

Adams, A. (2011). "Josh wears pink cleats": Inclusive masculinity on the soccer field. *Journal of Homosexuality* 58: 579–596.

Adams, A., and Anderson, E. (forthcoming). Homosexuality and sport: Exploring the influence of coming out to the teammates of a small, Midwestern Catholic college soccer team. *Sport, Education, and Society.*

Adams, A., Anderson, E., and McCormack, M. (2010). Establishing and challenging masculinity: The influence of gendered discourses in organized sport. *Journal of Language and Social Psychology* 29 (3): 278–300.

Agars, M. D., and Kottke, J. L. (2004). Models and practice of diversity management: A historical review and presentation of new integrated theory. In M. S. Stockdale and F. J. Crosby (eds.), *The psychology and management of workplace diversity* (pp. 55–77). Malden, MA: Blackwell.

Allison, T., and Symons, C. (2010). A funny and nice and stupid event: The Pink Flamingo relay. Unpublished paper presented at the annual conference of the North American Society for Sport History, Disneyworld Florida, May 27–31.

Allport, G. W. (1954). *The nature of prejudice.* Cambridge, MA: Addison-Wesley.

Altman, D. (1994). *Power and community: Organizational and cultural responses to AIDS.* London: Taylor and Francis.

Anderson, B. (1983). *Imagined communities: Reflections on the origin and spread of nationalism.* London: Verso.

Anderson, E. (2000). *Trailblazing: The true story of America's first openly gay high school coach.* Hollywood: Alyson.

—— (2002). Openly gay athletes: Contesting hegemonic masculinity in a homophobic environment. *Gender & Society* 16 (6): 860–877.

—— (2005a). *In the Game: Gay athletes and the cult of masculinity.* Albany: State University of New York Press.

—— (2005b). Orthodox and inclusive masculinity: Competing masculinities among heterosexual men in a feminized terrain. *Sociological Perspectives* 48 (3): 337–355.

—— (2008a). "I used to think women were weak": Orthodox masculinity, gender segregation, and sport. *Sociological Forum* 23 (2): 257–280.

—— (2008b). Inclusive masculinity in a fraternal setting. *Men and Masculinities* 10 (5): 604–620.

—— (2009). *Inclusive masculinity: The changing nature of masculinities.* London: Routledge.

—— (2010). *Sport, theory, and social problems: A critical introduction.* Abingdon, UK: Routledge.

—— (2011a). Masculinities and sexualities in sport and physical cultures: Three decades of evolving research. *Journal of Homosexuality* 58: 565–578.

—— (2011b). Updating the outcome: Gay athletes, straight teams, and coming out in educationally based sport teams. *Gender & Society* 25 (2): 250–268.

—— (forthcoming). Inclusive masculinity and soccer at a Catholic university in the American Midwest. *Gender and Education* iFirst: 1–18.

Anderson, E., Adams, A., and Rivers, I. (2010). "I kiss them because I love them": The emergence of heterosexual men kissing in British institutes of education. *Archives of Sexual Behaviors* iFirst: 1–10.

Anderson, E., and McCormack, M. (2010a). Comparing the black gay male athlete: Patterns in American oppression. *Journal of Men's Studies* 18 (2): 145–158.

—— (2010b). Intersectionality, critical race theory, and American sporting oppression: Examining black and gay male athletes. *Journal of Homosexuality* 57: 949–967.

Anderson, E., and McGuire, R. (2010). Inclusive masculinity theory and the politics of men's rugby. *Journal of Gender Studies* 19 (3): 249–262.

Arcordia, C., and Whitford, M. (2008). Festival attendance and the development of social capital. *Journal of Convention and Event Tourism* 8 (2): 1–18.

Aronson (2004). The threat of stereotype. *Education Leadership* 62: 14–19.

Ashmore, R. D., and Del Boca, F. K. (1979). Sex stereotypes and implicit personality theory: Toward a cognitive-social psychological conceptualization. *Sex Roles* 5: 219–248.

Asia Pacific Games (2011). Final report: 2nd Asia Pacific Outgames. March 12–19. Archived at Victoria University. Caroline Symons personal archive.

Associated Press (2010). Transgender Kye Allums to play for GW. November 5. http://sports.espn.go.com/ncw/news/story?id=5758450.

Avery, Derek R. (2011). Support for diversity in organizations. *Organizational Psychology Review* 1 (3): 239–256.

Azzarito, L., and Solomon, M. A. (2005). A reconceptualization of physical education: The intersection of gender/race/social class. *Sport, Education, and Society* 10: 25–47.

Bachman, R. (2011). Sherri Murrell, after four winning seasons at Portland State, still only publicly gay coach in D-I basketball. *The Oregonian*, July 19. http://www.oregonlive.com/vikings/index.ssf/2011/07/sherri_murrell_after_four_winn.html.

Bandura, A. (1986). *Social foundations for thought and action: A social cognitive theory.* Englewood Cliffs, NJ: Prentice-Hall.

BBC (British Broadcasting Corporation) (2009). In-depth interview: Gareth Thomas. http://news.bbc.co.uk/sport2/hi/rugby_union/welsh/8425335.stm.

Beasley, C. (2008). Rethinking hegemonic masculinity in a globalizing world. *Men and Masculinities* 11 (1): 86–103.

Beatty, J. E., and Kirby, S. L. (2006). Beyond the legal environment: How stigma influences invisible identity groups in the workplace. *Employee Responsibilities and Rights Journal* 18: 29–44.

Bell, M. P., Connerley, M. L., and Cocchiara, F. K. (2009). The case for mandatory diversity education. *Academy of Management Learning and Education* 8: 597–609.

Bernstein, M. (2004). Paths to homophobia. *Sexuality Research & Social Policy: A Journal of the NSRC* 1: 41–55.

Billman, J. (2004). Michelle raises hell. *Outside,* April.

Binder, J., Zagefka, H., Brown, R., Funke, F., Kessler, T., Mummendey, A., Maquil, A., Demoulin, S., and Leyens, J.-P. (2009). Does contact reduce prejudice or does prejudice reduce contact?

A longitudinal test of the contact hypothesis among majority and minority groups in three European countries. *Journal of Personality and Social Psychology* 96: 843–856.

Birrell, S., and Richter, D. (1987). Is a diamond forever? Feminist transformations of sport. *Women's Studies International Forum* 10 (4): 395–410.

Bondyopadhyay, A. (2002). Reflections on experiences of Sydney 2002. Online message to the AP Rainbow electronic mailing list. http://www.groups.yahoo.com/groups/ap-rainbo.

Bordo, S. (1993). *Unbearable weight: Feminism, Western culture, and the body.* Berkeley: University of California Press.

Borrie, S. (2003). Sydney 2002 Gay Games and Cultural Festival Sports Department final report. March. Archived at Victoria University. Caroline Symons personal archive.

Bosson, J. K., Haymovitz, E. L., and Pinel, E. C. (2004). When saying and doing diverge: The effects of stereotype threat on self-reported versus non-verbal anxiety. *Journal of Experimental Social Psychology* 40: 247–255.

Brackenridge, C., Allred, P., Jarvis, A., Maddocks, K., and Rivers, I. (2008). *A literature review of sexual orientation in sport.* London: Sport Scotland, Sport Northern Ireland, and UK Sport.

Brady, E. (2010a). At GW, transgender male playing for women's team. *USA Today,* November 4.

——— (2010b). Transgender male Kye Allums on the women's team at GW. *USA Today,* November 3. http://www.usatoday.com/sports/college/womensbasketball/atlantic10/2010-11-03-kye-allums-george-washington-transgender_N.htm.

Britton, D. M., and Williams, C. L. (1995). "Don't ask, don't tell, don't pursue": Military policy and the construction of heterosexual masculinity. *Journal of Homosexuality* 30 (1): 1–21.

Brooks, V. R. (1981). *Minority stress and lesbian women.* Lexington, MA: Heath.

Brown, R., and Hewstone, M. (2005). An integrative theory of intergroup contact. *Advances in Experimental Social Psychology* 37: 255–343.

Bruening, J. E. (2005). Gender and racial analysis in sport: Are all the women white and all the blacks men? *Quest* 57: 330–349.

Burton-Nelson, M. (1995). *The stronger women get the more men love football: Sexism and the American culture of sports.* New York: Avon.

Bush, A., Anderson, E., and Carr, S. (2012). The declining existence of men's homophobia in British sport. *Journal for the Study of Sports and Athletes in Education* 6: 107–120.

Butler, J. (1990). *Gender trouble: Feminism and the subversion of identity*. New York: Routledge.

Buzinski, J. (2005). Sheryl Swoopes comes out. October 26. http://www.outsports.com/women/20051026sherylswoopes.htm.

——— (2006). Gay Games vs Outgames. Discussion board, August. http://www.outsports.com/forrums/index.php.

Buzuvis, E. (2011). Transgender student-athletes and sex-segregated sports: Developing policies of inclusion for intercollegiate and interscholastic athletics. *Seton Hall Journal of Sports and Entertainment Law* 21: 1–60.

Califia, P. (1997). *Sex changes: The politics of transgenderism*. San Francisco: Cleis Press.

Calkins, M. (2008). Transgender golfer is women's long drive champ. *Press-Enterprise* (Riverside, CA), December 31.

Cameron, D., and Kulick, D. (2003). *Language and sexuality*. Cambridge: Cambridge University Press.

Carbery, G. (1995). *A history of the Sydney Gay and Lesbian Mardi Gras*. Melbourne: Australian Lesbian and Gay Archives.

Carlson, C. (1982). *The Voice* 4(18). September 10.

Cavanagh, L., and Sykes, H. (2006). Transsexual bodies at the Olympics: The International Olympic Committee's policy on transsexual athletes at the 2004 Athens Summer Games. *Body & Society* 12: 75–102.

Chandler, T., and Nauright, J. (1996). Introduction: Rugby, manhood, and identity. In J. Nauright and T. Chandler (eds.), *Making men: Rugby and masculine identity* (pp. 1–12). London: Cass.

Chelladurai, P. (2009). *Managing organizations for sport and physical activity: A systems perspective*. Scottsdale, AZ: Holcomb Hathaway.

City of New York (1996). Economic impact assessment for Gay Games IV and Cultural Festival. May 29. Archived at San Francisco Public Library. Federation of Gay Games Archive, Box 5, Series IV, Gay Games IV, Folder 32.

Clair, J. A., Beatty, J. E., and MacLean, T. L. (2005). Out of sight but not out of mind: Managing invisible social identities in the workplace. *Academy of Management Review* 30: 78–95.

Coakley, J. (2009). *Sports in society: Issues and controversies*. 10th ed. Boston: McGraw-Hill.

Coe, R. (1986). *A sense of pride: The story of Gay Games II*. San Francisco: Pride Publications.

Conley, T. D., Devine, P. G., Rabow, J., and Evett, S. R. (2002). Gay men and lesbians' experiences in and expectations for interactions with heterosexuals. *Journal of Homosexuality* 44: 83–109.

Connell, R. W. (1987). *Gender and power.* Stanford: Stanford University Press.

———— (1995). *Masculinities.* Berkeley: University of California Press.

Connell, R. W., and Messerschmidt, J. (2005). Hegemonic masculinity: Rethinking the concept. *Gender & Society* 19 (6): 829–859.

Couch, M., Pitts, M., Mulcare, H., Croy, S., Mitchell, A., and Patel, S. (2007). *TranZnation: A report on the health and wellbeing of transgendered people in Australia and New Zealand.* Melbourne: Latrobe University, Gay and Lesbian Health Victoria, and the Australian Centre on Sex, Health, and Society.

Crenshaw, K. (1989). Demarginalizing the intersection of race and sex: A black feminist critique of antidiscrimination doctrine, feminist theory, and antiracist politics. *University of Chicago Legal Forum*: 139–167.

———— (1991). Mapping the margins: Intersectionality, identity politics, and violence against women of color. *Stanford Law Review* 43: 1241–1299.

Crincoli, S. (2011). Eligibility: The IAAF hyperandrogenism regulations and discrimination. *World Sports Law Report* 9 (6). http://www.e-comlaw.com/wslr/archive/volume_9_issue_6.htm.

Crocker, J., and Major, B. (1989). Social stigma and self-esteem: The self-protective properties of stigma. *Psychological Review* 96: 608–630.

Crocker, J., Major, B., and Steele, C. (1998). Social stigma. In D. T. Gilbert and S. T. Fiske (eds.), *The handbook of social psychology* (pp. 504–553). Boston: McGraw-Hill.

Cryer, B., McCraty, R., and Childre, D. (2003). Pull the plug on stress. *Harvard Business Review* 81 (7): 102.

Cunningham, G. B. (2008a). Commitment to diversity and its influence on athletic department outcomes. *Journal of Intercollegiate Sport* 1: 176–201.

———— (2008b). Creating and sustaining gender diversity in sport organizations. *Sex Roles* 58: 136–145.

———— (2009). Understanding the diversity-related change process: A field study. *Journal of Sport Management* 23: 407–428.

———— (2010a). Demographic dissimilarity and affective reactions to physical activity classes: The moderating effects of diversity beliefs. *International Journal of Sport Psychology* 41: 387–402.

——— (2010b). Predictors of sexual orientation diversity in intercollegiate athletics. *Journal of Intercollegiate Sport* 3: 256–269.

——— (2010c). Understanding the underrepresentation of African American coaches: A multilevel perspective. *Sport Management Review* 13: 395–406.

——— (2011a). Creative work environments in sport organizations: The influence of sexual orientation diversity and commitment to diversity. *Journal of Homosexuality* 58: 1041–1057.

——— (2011b). The LGBT advantage: Examining the relationship among sexual orientation diversity, diversity strategy, and performance. *Sport Management Review* 14: 453–461.

Cunningham, G. B., and Fink, J. S. (2006). Diversity issues in sport and leisure: Introduction to a special issue. *Journal of Sport Management* 20: 455–465.

Cunningham, G. B., and Fitzgerald, A. O. (2006). The influence of message content on reactions to Title IX. *Applied Research in Coaching and Athletics Annual* 21: 238–258.

Cunningham, G. B., and Melton, E. N. (2011). The benefits of sexual orientation diversity in sport organizations. *Journal of Homosexuality* 58: 647–663.

Cunningham, G. B., and Sagas, M. (2005). Access discrimination in intercollegiate athletics. *Journal of Sport and Social Issues* 29: 148–163.

Cunningham, G. B., and Sartore, M. L. (2010). Championing diversity: The influence of personal and organizational antecedents. *Journal of Applied Social Psychology* 40 (4): 788–810.

Cunningham, G. B., Sartore, M. L., and McCullough, B. P. (2010). The influence of applicant sexual orientation and rater sex on ascribed attributions and hiring recommendations of personal trainers. *Journal of Sport Management* 24: 400–415.

Cunningham, G. B., and Singer, J. N. (2009). *Diversity in athletics: An assessment of exemplars and institutional best practices.* Indianapolis: National Collegiate Athletic Association.

——— (2010). "You'll face discrimination wherever you go": Student athletes' intentions to enter the coaching profession. *Journal of Applied Social Psychology* 40 (7): 1708–1727.

Cyphers, L., and Fagan, K. (2011). Homophobia and recruiting. *ESPN Magazine*, January 26. http://sports.espn.go.com/ncw/news/story?id=6060641.

Daniels, E. A. (2009). Sex objects, athletes, and sexy athletes. *Journal of Adolescent Research* 24 (4): 399.

Davies, J. (1962). Toward a theory of revolution. *American Sociological Review* 27: 5–19.

Davies, P. G., Spencer, S. J., and Steele, C. M. (2005). Clearing the air: Identity safety moderates the effects of stereotype threat on women's leadership aspirations. *Journal of Personality and Social Psychology* 88: 276–287.

Davis, A. (2006). The Gay Games begin . . . continuing coverage. July 19. http://www.windycitymediagroup.com.

Day, N. E., and Greene, P. G. (2008). A case for sexual orientation diversity management in small and large organizations. *Human Resource Management* 47: 637–654.

DeHass, D. (2009). *2007–08 ethnic and gender demographics of NCAA member institutions' athletic personnel.* Indianapolis: National Collegiate Athletic Association.

DePalma, R., and Jennett, M. (2010). Homophobia, transphobia, and culture: Deconstructing heteronormativity in English primary schools. *Intercultural Education* 21 (1): 15–26.

DeRolf, S. (1997). *The crayon box that talked.* New York: Scholastic.

DeSensi, J. T. (1995). Understanding multiculturalism and valuing diversity: A theoretical perspective. *Quest* 47: 34–43.

Devine, P. G. (1989). Stereotypes and prejudice: Their automatic and controlled components. *Journal of Personality and Social Psychology* 56: 5–18.

Devries, M. (2008). Do transitioned athletes compete at an advantage or disadvantage? Promising Practices: Working with Transitioning/Transitioned Athletes in Sport Project. http://www.caaws.ca/e/resources/article.cfm?id=2519.

DGQ Media Inc. (2006). Montreal 2006: Official program of the international conference on LGBT human rights of the 1st World Outgames. Archived at Victoria University. Caroline Symons personal archive.

DiPlacido, J. (1998). Minority stress among lesbians, gay men, and bisexuals: A consequence of heterosexism, homophobia, and stigmatization. In G. M. Herek (ed.), *Psychological perspectives on lesbian and gay issues,* vol. 4, *Stigma and sexual orientation: Understanding prejudice against lesbians, gay men, and bisexuals* (pp. 138–159). Thousand Oaks, CA: Sage.

Doherty, A. J., and Chelladurai, P. (1999). Managing cultural diversity in sport organizations: A theoretical perspective. *Journal of Sport Management* 13: 280–297.

Dovidio, J. F., Brigham, J. C., Johnson, B. T., and Gaertner, S. L. (1996). Stereotyping, prejudice, and discrimination: Another look. In N. Macrae, C. Stangor, and M. Hewstone (eds.), *Stereotypes and stereotyping* (pp. 276–319). New York: Guilford.

Dowling, C. (2000). *The frailty myth: Redefining the physical potential of women and girls.* New York: Random.

Dreger, A. (2010). Sex typing for sport. *The Hastings Center Report* 40: 22–24.

Dworkin, S. H., and Yi, H. (2003). LGBT identity, violence, and social justice: The psychological is political. *International Journal for the Advancement of Counseling,* 25: 269–279.

Eccles, J. S., Jacobs, J. E., and Harold, R. D. (1990). Gender role stereotypes, expectancy effects, and parents' socialization of gender differences. *Journal of Social Issues* 46 (2): 183–201.

Eitzen, D. S., and Sage, G. H. (2003). *Sociology of North American sport.* 7th ed. New York: McGraw-Hill.

Eliason, M., Donelan, C., and Randall, C. (1992). Lesbian stereotypes. *Health Care for Women International* 13: 131–144.

Ellings, A., De Knop, P., and Knoppers, A. (2003). Gay/lesbian sports clubs and events: Places for homo-social bonding and cultural resistance? *International Review for the Sociology of Sport* 38 (4): 441–456.

Ely, R. J., and Thomas, D. A. (2001). Cultural diversity at work: The effects of diversity perspectives on work group processes and outcomes. *Administrative Science Quarterly* 46: 229–273.

Ezzell, M. B. (2009). "Barbie Dolls" on the pitch: Identity work, defensive othering, and inequality in women's rugby. *Social Problems* 56: 111–131.

Farrar, S. (2002). This sporting strife: Games loss hurts small business. *Sydney Star Observer,* December 12.

Fausto-Sterling, A. (2000). *Sexing the body: Gender politics and the construction of sexuality.* New York: Basic.

Feinberg, L. (1996). *Transgender warriors: Making history, from Joan of Arc to Dennis Rodman.* Boston: Beacon.

Fingerhut, A. W., Peplau, L. A., and Gable, S. L. (2010). Identity, minority stress, and psychological well-being among gay men and lesbians. *Psychology and Sexuality* 1: 101–114.

Fink, J. S., Burton, L. J., Farrell, A. O., and Parker, H. M. (2012). Playing it out: Female intercollegiate athletes' experiences in revealing their sexual identities. *Journal for the Study of Sports and Athletes in Education* 6: 83–106.

Fink, J. S., and Pastore, D. L. (1999). Diversity in sport? Utilizing the business literature to devise a comprehensive framework of diversity initiatives. *Quest* 51: 310–327.

Fink, J. S., Pastore, D. L., and Riemer, H. A. (2001). Do differences make a difference? Managing diversity in Division IA intercollegiate athletics. *Journal of Sport Management* 15: 10–50.

—— (2003). Managing employee diversity: Perceived practices and organizational outcomes in NCAA Division III athletic departments. *Sport Management Review* 6: 147–168.

Fiske, S. T. (1998). Stereotyping, prejudice, and discrimination. In D. T. Gilbert, and S. T. Fiske (eds.), *The handbook of social psychology,* vol. 2 (pp. 357–411). Boston: McGraw-Hill.

Florida, R. (2002). The economic geography of talent. *Annals of the Association of American Geographers* 92: 743–755.

—— (2003). Cities and the creative class. *City & Community* 2: 3–19.

—— (2004). *The rise of the creative class: And how it's transforming work, leisure, community, and everyday life.* New York: Basic.

Flowers, P., and Buston, K. (2001). "I was terrified of being different": Exploring gay men's accounts of growing up in a heterosexist society. *Journal of Adolescence* 24: 51–65.

Freedman, E. (1995). The historical construction of homosexuality in the U.S. *Socialist Review* 25: 31–46.

Friend, R. A. (1991). Older lesbian and gay people: A theory of successful aging. *Journal of Homosexuality* 20 (3–4): 99–118.

Gay Games IV and Cultural Festival (1994). Athlete registration book. New York.

Geertz, C. (1973). *The interpretation of cultures: Selected essays.* London: Fontana.

Gilbert, J. A., and Ivancevich, J. M. (2000). Valuing diversity: A tale of two organizations. *Academy of Management Executive* 14 (1): 93–105.

Gill, D. L., Morrow, R. G., Collins, K. E., Lucey, A. B., and Schultz, A. M. (2006). Attitudes and sexual prejudice in sport and physical activity. *Journal of Sport Management* 20: 554–564.

Goffman, E. (1963). *Stigma: Notes on the management of spoiled identity.* Englewood Cliffs, NJ: Prentice-Hall.

Gosiorek, J. C., and Weinrich, J. D. (1991). The definition and scope of sexual orientation. In J. C. Gonsiorek and J. D. Weinrich (eds.), *Homosexuality: Research implications for public policy* (pp. 1–12). Newbury Park, CA: Sage.

Gramsci, A. (1971). *Selections from prison notebooks.* London: New Left.

Granderson, L. Z. (2005). Three-time MVP "tired of having to hide my feelings." *ESPN Magazine,* October 27. http://sports.espn.go .com/wnba/news/story?id=2203853.

Green, N. (1988). Sodomite invasion planned for 1990. *Life Gazette,* October 1.

Greene, B. (2000). African American lesbian and bisexual women. *Journal of Social Issues* 56 (2): 239–249.

Griffin, P. (1992). Changing the game: Homophobia, sexism, and lesbians in sport. *Quest* 44: 251–265.

——— (1998). *Strong women, deep closets: Lesbians and homophobia in sport.* Champaign, IL: Human Kinetics.

——— (2007). Women's basketball coaches need to step up against homophobia. *Pat Griffin's LGBT Sport Blog,* April 3. http:// ittakesateam.blogspot.com/2007/04/womens-basketball-coaches-need-to-step.html.

Griffin, P., and Carroll, H. (2010). On the team: Equal opportunities for transgender student athletes. National Center for Lesbian Rights and Women's Sports Foundation. http://www.nclrights.org /site/DocServer/TransgenderStudentAthleteReport.pdf?docID =7901.

Handley, M. (2010). The IOC grapples with Olympic sex testing. *Time World.* http://www.time.com/time/world/article/0,8599,196 3333,00.html#ixzz1Vm11BY96.

Hargreaves, J. (2000). *Heroines of sport: The politics of difference and identity.* London: Routledge.

Harry, J. (1995). Sports ideology, attitudes toward women, and anti-homosexual attitudes. *Sex Roles* 32: 109–116.

Hart, S. (2010). Caster Semenya's dominant 800 metres victory in Berlin unleashes gender storm. *Daily Telegraph,* August 22.

Hartmann, H. (1976). Capitalism, patriarchy, and job segregation. *Signs: Journal of Women in Culture and Society* 1 (3): 137–169.

Hebl, M. R., Foster, J. B., Mannix, L. M., and Dovidio, J. F. (2002). Formal and interpersonal discrimination: A field study of bias toward homosexual applicants. *Personality and Social Psychology Bulletin* 28: 815–825.

Hekma, G. (1998). "As long as they don't make an issue of it . . .": Gay men and lesbians in organized sports in the Netherlands. *Journal of Homosexuality* 35 (1): 1–23.

Herek, G. M. (1988). Heterosexuals' attitudes toward lesbians and gay men: Correlates and gender differences. *Journal of Sex Research* 25: 451–477.

—— (2000). The psychology of sexual prejudice. *Current Directions in Psychological Science* 9: 19–22.

—— (2002). Heterosexuals' attitudes toward bisexual men and women in the United States. *Journal of Sex Research* 39 (4): 264–274.

—— (2004). Beyond "homophobia": Thinking about sexual prejudice and stigma in the twenty-first century. *Journal of the National Sexuality Resource Center* 1: 6–24.

—— (2007). Confronting sexual stigma and prejudice: Theory and practice. *Journal of Social Issues* 63 (4): 905–925.

—— (2009). Sexual stigma and sexual prejudice in the United States: A conceptual framework. In D. A. Hope (ed.), *Contemporary perspectives on lesbian, gay, and bisexual identities: The 54th Nebraska Symposium on Motivation* (pp. 65–111). New York: Springer.

Herek, G. M., and Capitanio, J. P. (1999). Sex differences in how heterosexuals think about lesbians and gay men: Evidence from survey context effects. *Journal of Sex Research* 36: 348–360.

Herek, G. M., and Garnets, L. D. (2007). Sexual orientation and mental health. *Annual Review of Clinical Psychology* 3: 353–375.

Herek, G. M., Gillis, J. R., and Cogan, J. C. (2009). Internalized stigma among sexual minority adults: Insights from a social psychological perspective. *Journal of Counseling Psychology* 56 (1): 32.

Hewstone, M., and Brown, R. (1986). Contact is not enough: An intergroup perspective on the "contact hypothesis." In M. Hewstone and R. Brown (eds.), *Contact and conflict in intergroup encounters* (pp. 1–44). Oxford: Blackwell.

Homan, A. C., van Knippenberg, D., Van Kleef, G. A., and De Dreu, C. K. W. (2007). Bridging faultlines by valuing diversity: Diversity beliefs, information elaboration, and performance in diverse work groups. *Journal of Applied Psychology* 92: 1189–1199.

Howson, R. (2006). *Challenging hegemonic masculinity.* London: Routledge.

Huffman, A. H., Watrous-Rodriguez, K. M., and King, E. B. (2008). Supporting a diverse workforce: What type of support is most meaningful for lesbian and gay employees? *Human Resource Management* 47: 237–253.

IAAF (International Amateur Athletics Federation) (2011). Regulations governing eligibility of females with hyperandrogenism to compete in women's competition. http://www.iaaf.org/mm /Document/Medical/PolicyStmnts&Adv/05/99/96/201105120337 10_httppostedfile_IAAFRegulationsGoverningEligibilityof FemaleswithHyperandrogenismtoCompeteinWomen%E2%80%9 9sCompetition_24481.pdf

Iannotta, J. G., and Kane, M. J. (2002). Sexual stories as resistance narratives in women's sports: Reconceptualizing identity performance. *Sociology of Sport Journal* 19: 347–369.

IOC (International Olympic Committee) (2003). Statement on the Stockholm Consensus on sex reassignment in sport. http://www .olympic.org/Documents/Reports/EN/en_report_905.pdf.

Jayne, M. E. A., and Dipboye, R. L. (2004). Leveraging diversity to improve business performance: Research findings and recommendations for organizations. *Human Resource Management* 43: 409–424.

Kalev, A., Dobbin, F., and Kelly, E. (2006). Best practices or best guesses? Assessing the efficacy of corporate affirmative action and diversity policies. *American Sociological Review* 71: 589–617.

Kandel, D. B., and Andrews, K. (2009). Processes of adolescent socialization by parents and peers. July 3. http://informahealth care.com/doi/abs/10.3109/10826088709027433.

Kane, M. J. (1988). Media coverage of the female athlete before, during, and after Title IX: *Sports Illustrated* revisited. *Journal of Sport Management* 2: 87–99.

Kian, E. M., and Anderson, E. (2009). John Amaechi: Changing the way sport reporters examine gay athletes. *Journal of Homosexuality* 56: 799–818.

Kiesling, S. F. (2007). Men, masculinities, and language. *Language and Linguistics Compass* 1 (6): 653–673.

Kimmel, M. S. (1994). Masculinity as homophobia: Fear, shame, and silence in the construction of gender identity. In H. Brod and M. Kaufman (eds.), *Theorising masculinities* (pp. 213–219). London: Sage.

King, J. R. (2004). The (im)possibility of gay teachers for young children. *Theory Into Practice* 43: 122–127.

Kitsantas, A. (2004). Studying abroad: The role of college students' goals on the development of cross-cultural skills and global understanding. *College Student Journal* 38: 441–452.

Knoppers, A., Bedker-Meyer, B., Ewing, M., and Forrest, L. (1990). Dimensions of Power: A question of sport or gender? *Sociology of Sport Journal* 7: 369–377.

———— (1991). Opportunity and work behavior in college coaching. *Journal of Sport and Social Issues* 15: 1–20.

Kolnes, L. J. (1995). Heterosexuality as an organizing principle in women's sport. *International Review for Sociology of Sport* 30: 61–77.

Kozlowski, S. W. J., and Klein, K. J. (2000). A multilevel approach to theory and research in organizations: Contextual, temporal, and emergent processes. In K. J. Klein and S. W. J. Kozlowski (eds.), *Multilevel theory, research, and methods in organizations: Foundations, extensions, and new directions* (pp. 3–90). San Francisco: Jossey-Bass.

Krane, V. (1997). Homonegativism experienced by lesbian collegiate athletes. *Women in Sport & Physical Activity Journal* 6: 141–164.

———— (2001). We can be athletic and feminine, but do we want to? Challenging hegemonic femininity in sport. *Quest* 53: 115–133.

Krane, V., and Barber, H. (2003). Lesbian experience in sport: A social identity perspective. *Quest* 55: 328–346.

———— (2005). Identity tensions in lesbian intercollegiate coaches. *Research Quarterly for Exercise and Sport* 76: 67–81.

Krane, V., Barber H., and McClung, L. R. (2002). Social psychological benefits of Gay Games participation: A social identity theory explanation. *Journal of Applied Sport Psychology* 14: 27–42.

Krane, V., Choi, P. Y. L., Baird, S. M., Aimar, C. M., and Kauer, K. J. (2004). Living the paradox: Female athletes negotiate femininity and muscularity. *Sex roles* 50 (5): 315–329.

Krane, V., and Romont, L. (1997). Female athletes' motives and experiences at the Gay Games. *Journal of Gay, Lesbian, and Bisexual Identities* 2: 123–138.

Krane, V., Ross, S. R., Miller, M., Rowse, J. L., Ganoe, K., Andrzejczyk, J. A., and Lucas, C. B. (2010). Power and focus: self-representation of female college athletes. *Qualitative Research in Sport and Exercise* 2 (2): 175–195.

Kulik, C. T., and Roberson, L. (2008). Common goals and golden opportunities: Evaluations of diversity education in academic and organizational settings. *Academy of Management Learning & Education* 7: 309–331.

Labreque, L. (ed.) (1994). *Unity: A celebration of Gay Games IV and Stonewall.* San Francisco: Labreque Publishers.

Lalor, T., and Rendle-Short, J. (2007). "That's so gay": A contemporary use of *gay* in Australian English. *Australian Journal of Linguistics* 27 (2): 147–173.

Lapchick, R. (2010a). *The 2010 racial and gender report card—NBA*. Orlando: University of Central Florida, Institute for Diversity and Ethics in Sport.

———— (2010b). *The 2010 racial and gender report card—WNBA*. Orlando: University of Central Florida, Institute for Diversity and Ethics in Sport.

LeVay, S. (2010). *Gay, straight, and the reason why: The science of sexual orientation.* New York: Oxford University Press.

Lewis, G. B. (2003). Black-white differences in attitudes toward homosexuality and gay rights. *Public Opinion Quarterly* 67: 59–78.

Lewis, R. J., Derlega, V. J., Clarke, E. G., and Kuang, J. C. (2006). Stigma consciousness, social constraints, and lesbian well-being. *Journal of Counseling Psychology* 53: 48–56.

Lindsey, E. W. (2005). Study abroad and value development in social work students. *Journal of Social Work Education* 41: 229–249.

Link, B. G., and Phelan, J. C. (2001). Conceptualizing stigma. *Annual Review of Sociology* 27: 363–385.

Litchfield, C., and Symons, C. (2011). "Hockey one, hockey two, hockey three": Participation, inclusion, and policy at three community hockey clubs in Victoria. In M. Burke, C. Hanlon, and C. Thomen (eds.), *Sport, culture, and society: Approaches, methods, and perspectives* (pp. 127–142). Melbourne: Maribyrnong Press.

Loftus, J. (2001). America's liberalization in attitudes towards homosexuality, 1973–1998. *American Sociological Review* 66: 762–782.

Lubensky, M. E., Holland, S. L., Wiethoff, C., and Crosby, F. J. (2004). Diversity and sexual orientation: Including and valuing sexual minorities in the workplace. In M. S. Stockdale and F. J. Crosby (eds.), *The psychology and management of workplace diversity* (pp. 206–223). Malden, MA: Blackwell.

Lytton, H. (2000). Toward a model of family-environmental and child-biological influences on development. *Developmental Review* 20: 150–179.

Major, B., and O'Brien, L. T. (2005). The social psychology of stigma. *Annual Review of Psychology* 56: 393–421.

Major, B., Spencer, S., Schmader, T., Wolfe, C., and Crocker, J. (1998). Coping with negative stereotypes about intellectual performance: The role of psychological disengagement. *Personality and social psychology bulletin* 24: 34–50.

Marchant, J. (2011). Women with high male hormone levels face sport ban. *Nature News.* http://www.nature.com/news/2011 /110414/full/news.2011.237.html.

McCormack, M. (2011a). The declining significance of homohysteria for male students in three sixth forms in the south of England. *British Educational Research Journal* 37 (2): 337–353.

——— (2011b). Hierarchy without hegemony: Locating boys in an inclusive masculinity school setting. *Sociological Perspectives* 54 (1): 83–101.

——— (2011c). Mapping the terrain of homosexually-themed language. *Journal of Homosexuality* 58 (5): 664–679.

——— (2012). *The declining significance of homophobia: How teenage boys are redefining masculinity and heterosexuality.* New York: Oxford University Press.

McCormack, M., and Anderson, E. (2010a). "It's just not acceptable any more": The erosion of homophobia and the softening of masculinity at an English sixth form. *Sociology* 44 (5): 843–859.

——— (2010b). The re-production of homosexually-themed discourse in educationally-based organized sport. *Culture, Health, & Sexuality* 12 (8): 913–927.

McDonagh, E., and Pappano, L. (2008). *Playing with the boys: Why separate is not equal in sports.* New York: Oxford University Press.

McDonald, J. (2011). Hanging with the bats: Exploring the experiences of players from a "lesbian" soccer club in Australia. Unpublished honors thesis, University of Western Sydney, School of Humanities and Languages.

McDowell, J., and Cunningham, G. B. (2009). Personal, social, and organizational factors that influence black female athletic administrators' identity negotiation. *Quest* 61: 202–222.

McKindra, L. (2006). Transgender cases present challenge for policymakers. *NCAA News.* http://www.nclrights.org/site/PageServer ?pagename=issue_sports_spncaanewsonline112006.

Melbourne Outgames Inc. (2008). *Summary evaluation report.* Archived at Victoria University. Caroline Symons personal archive.

Melton, E. N. (2010a). Queer eye for the straight guy? The effects of LGBT-inclusive policies on organizational attraction. Paper presented at the annual conference of the North American Society for Sport Management, Tampa, FL, June.

——— (2010b). Sport and media. In G. B. Cunningham and J. N.

Singer (eds.), *Sociology of sport and physical activity* (pp. 103–134). College Station, TX: Center for Sport Management Research and Education.

Melton, E. N., and Cunningham, G. B. (2012). When identities collide: Exploring minority stress and resilience among college athletes with multiple marginalized identities. *Journal for the Study of Sports and Athletes in Education* 6: 45–65.

—— (forthcoming). Examining the experiences of LGBT sport employees: A social categorization theory perspective. *Journal of Sport Management.*

Melton, E. N., Cunningham, G. B., and McCullough, B. P. (2010). "LGBT-friendly brand positioning." Paper presented at the annual conference of the Sport Marketing Association, New Orleans, LA, November.

Messner, M. A. (1988). Sports and male domination: The female athlete as contested ideological terrain. *Sociology of Sport Journal* 5: 197–211.

—— (1992). *Power at play: Sport and the problem of masculinity.* Boston: Beacon.

—— (1994). Gay athletes and the Gay Games: An interview with Tom Waddell. In M. Messner and D. Sabo, *Sex, violence, and power in sport: Rethinking masculinity* (pp. 113–119). Freedom, CA: Crossing Press.

—— (2002). *Taking the field: Women, men, and sports.* Minneapolis: University of Minnesota Press.

Messner, M. A., and Sabo, D. F. (eds.) (1990). *Sport, men, and the gender order: Critical feminist perspectives.* Champaign, IL: Human Kinetics.

Meyer, I. H. (1995). Minority stress and mental health in gay men. *Journal of Health and Social Behavior* 36: 38–56.

—— (2001). Why lesbian, gay, bisexual, and transsexual public health? *American Journal of Public Health* 91: 856–859.

—— (2003). Prejudice, social stress, and mental health in lesbian, gay, and bisexual populations: Conceptual issues and research evidence. *Psychological Bulletin* 129: 674–697.

Meyer, J. W., and Rowan, B. (1977). Institutionalized organizations: Formal structure as myth and ceremony. *American Journal of Sociology* 83: 340–363.

Miles, D. (2011). Officials expect smooth "don't ask, don't tell" repeal. American Forces Press Service, September 20. http://www.af.mil/news/story.asp?id=123272723.

Milliken, F. J., and Martins, L. L. (1996). Searching for common threads: Understanding the multiple effects of diversity in organizational groups. *Academy of Management Review* 21 (2): 402–433.

Morris, J. (2006). Transgendered racer insulted; second-place finisher wears t-shirt "100 Per Cent Pure Woman Champ." *The Spectator* (Hamilton, Ontario), August 3.

Movement Advancement Project (2012). Talking about suicide and LGBT populations. www.lgbtmap.org/talking-about-suicide.

MVA&AA (Metropolitan Vancouver Arts & Athletic Association) (1990). Media release by Celebration '90. Archived at San Francisco Public Library. Federation of Gay Games Archive, Box 1, Series III, Gay Games III, Folder 1.

NCAA (National Collegiate Athletic Association) (2011). NCAA inclusion of transgender student-athletes. August. http://www.ncaa .org/wps/wcm/connect/fd9a78804841ff93953f9fbf5e8bc9cc /Transgender_Handbook_2011_Final.pdf?MOD=AJPERES&CA CHEID=fd9a78804841ff93953f9fbf5e8bc9cc.

Norman, L. 2010. Feeling second best: Elite women coaches' experiences. *Sociology of Sport Journal* 27: 89–104.

Norton, A. T., and Herek, G. M. (2012). Heterosexuals' attitudes toward transgender people: Findings from a national probability sample of U.S. adults. *Sex Roles.*

Ogburn, W. F. (1950). *On culture and social change.* Chicago: Chicago University Press.

Pascoe, C. J. (2005). "Dude, you're a fag": Adolescent masculinity and the fag discourse. *Sexualities* 8: 329–346.

Passa, D. (2005). Female golfer, once male, makes debut. *Pittsburgh Post-Gazette,* February 27.

Pastrana, A. (2006). The intersectional imagination: What do lesbian and gay leaders of color have to do with it? *Race, Gender, & Class* 13: 218–238.

Peterson, G. (2011). Clubbing masculinities: Gender shifts in gay men's dance floor choreographies. *Journal of Homosexuality* 58 (5): 608–625.

Peterson, G., and Anderson, E. (2012). The performance of softer masculinities on the university dance floor. *Journal of Men's Studies* 20 (1): 3–15.

Pettigrew, T. F. (1998). Intergroup contact theory. *Annual Review of Psychology* 49: 65–85.

Pettigrew, T. F., and Tropp, L. R. (2006). A meta-analytic test of intergroup contact theory. *Journal of Personality and Social Psychology* 90: 751–783.

Pinel, E. C. (1999). Stigma consciousness: The psychological legacy of social stereotypes. *Journal of Personality and Social Psychology* 76: 114–128.

Pinel, E. C., and Paulin, N. (2005). Stigma consciousness at work. *Basic and Applied Social Psychology* 27: 345–352.

Plummer, D. (1999). *One of the boys: Masculinity, homophobia, and modern manhood.* New York: Harrington Park.

———— (2006). Sportophobia: Why do some men avoid sport? *Journal of Sport and Social Issues* 30: 122–137.

Plymire, D. C., and Forman, P. J. (2000). Breaking the silence: Lesbian fans, the Internet, and the sexual politics of women's sport. *International Journal of Sexuality and Gender Studies* 5 (2): 141–153.

Price, M. (2000). Rugby as a gay men's game. Unpublished dissertation, University of Warwick.

Pronger, B. (1990). *The arena of masculinity: Sports, homosexuality, and the meaning of sex.* New York: St. Martin's.

Pugh, S. D., Dietz, J., Brief, A. P., and Wiley, J. W. (2008). Looking inside and out: The impact of employee and community demographic composition on organizational diversity climate. *Journal of Applied Psychology* 93: 1422–1428.

Ragins, B. R., Singh, R., and Cornwell, J. M. (2007). Making the invisible visible: Fear and disclosure of sexual orientation at work. *Journal of Applied Psychology* 4: 1103–1118.

Rasmussen, M. L. (2004). "That's so gay!": A study of the deployment of signifiers of sexual and gender identity in secondary school settings in Australia and the United States. *Social Semiotics* 14 (3): 289–308.

Reeser, J. C. (2005). Gender identity and sport: Is the playing field level? *British Journal of Sports Medicine* 39: 695–699.

Rich, A. (1980). Compulsory heterosexuality and lesbian existence. *Signs: A Journal of Women in Culture and Society* 5: 631–660.

Ritchie, R., Reynard, J., and Lewis, T. (2008). Intersex and the Olympic Games. *Journal of the Royal Society of Medicine* 101: 395–399.

Robinson G., and Dechant K. 1997. Building a business case for diversity. *Academy of Management Executive* 11 (3): 21–31.

Rotella, R. J., and Murray, M. M. (1991). Homophobia, the world of sport, and sport psychology consulting. *The Sport Psychologist* 5: 355–364.

Rowley, S. J., Kurtz-Costes, B., Mistry, R., and Feagans, L. (2007). Social status as a predictor of race and gender stereotypes in late childhood and early adolescence. *Social Development* 16: 150–168.

Rush, L. L. (1998). Affective reactions to multiple social stigmas. *Journal of Social Psychology* 138: 421–430.

Sage, G. H. (1998). *Power and ideology in American sport.* Champaign, IL: Human Kinetics.

Salamone, F. (2000). *Society, culture, leisure, and play: An anthropological reference.* Lanham, MD: University Press of America.

Sartore, M. L., and Cunningham, G. B. (2009a). Gender, sexual prejudice, and sport participation: Implications for sexual minorities. *Sex Roles* 60 (1): 100–113..

———— (2009b). The lesbian stigma in the sport context: Implications for women of every sexual orientation. *Quest* 61 (3): 289–305.

———— (2010). The lesbian label as a component of women's stigmatization in sport organizations: An exploration of two health and kinesiology departments. *Journal of Sport Management* 24: 481–501.

Sartore-Baldwin, M. L. (2012). Lesbian, gay, bisexual, and transgender athletes in sport: An interview with Pat Griffin. *Journal for the Study of Sports and Athletes in Education* 6: 141–151.

Savin-Williams, R. C. (2005). *The new gay teenager.* London: Harvard University Press.

Schein, E. H. (1990). Organizational culture. *American psychologist* 45 (2): 109.

Schmalz, D. L., and Kerstetter, D. L. (2006). Girlie girls and manly men: Children's stigma consciousness of gender in sports and physical activities. *Journal of Leisure Research* 38: 537–557.

———— (2008). Stigma consciousness as a predictor of children's participation in recreational vs. competitive sports. *Journal of Sport Behavior* 31: 276–297.

Scott, W. R. (2005). Institutional theory: Contributing to a theoretical research program. In K. G. Smith and M. A. Hitt (eds.), *Great minds in management: The process of theory development* (pp. 460–484). Oxford: Oxford University Press.

Shakib, S., and Dunbar, M. D. (2004). How high school athletes talk about maternal and paternal sporting experiences. *International Review for the Sociology of Sport* 39 (3): 275.

Shaw, S., and Hoeber, L. (2003). "A strong man is direct and a direct woman is a bitch": Gendered discourses and their influence on employment roles in sport organizations. *Journal of Sport Management* 17: 347–375.

Sidanius, J., Levin, S., Federico, C., and Pratto, F. (2001). Legitimizing ideologies: The social dominance approach. In J. T. Jost and B. Major (eds.), *The psychology of legitimacy: Emerging perspectives on ideology, justice, and intergroup relations* (pp. 307–331). New York: Cambridge University Press.

Simon, A. (1998). The relationship between stereotypes of and attitudes toward lesbians and gays. In G. M. Herek (ed.), *Psychological perspectives on lesbian and gay issues,* vol. 4, *Stigma and sexual orientation: Understanding prejudice against lesbians, gay men, and bisexuals* (pp. 62–81). Thousand Oaks, CA: Sage.

Simpson, J. L., Ljungqvist, A., and Ferguson-Smith, M. A. (2000). Gender verification in the Olympics. *Journal of the American Medical Association* 284 (12): 1568–1569.

Singer, J. N. (2005). Addressing epistemological racism in sport management research. *Journal of Sport Management* 19: 464–479.

Smith, D. (2009). Caster Semenya row: "Who are white people to question the makeup of an African girl? It is racism." *The Observer,* August 22.

Smith, G. (2010). Gareth Thomas . . . the only openly gay male athlete. *Sports Illustrated,* May 3. http://sportsillustrated.cnn.com/vault/article/magazine/MAG1168953/index.htm.

Smith, N. G., and Ingram, K. M. (2004). Workplace heterosexism and adjustment among lesbian, gay, and bisexual sexual minorities: The role of unsupportive social interactions. *Journal of Counseling Psychology* 51: 57–67.

Snyder, K. (2006). *The G quotient: Why gay executives are excelling as leaders . . . and what every manager needs to know.* San Francisco: Jossey-Bass.

Southall, R., Anderson, E., Southall, C., Nagel, M., and Polite, F. (2011). An investigation of the relationship between college athletes' ethnicity and sexual-orientation attitudes. *Ethnic and Racial Studies* 34: 293–313.

Sowers, P. (1994). Think pink. *Gay Games IV Aquatics Program:* 30–31.

Spencer, S. J., Steele, C. M., and Quinn, D. M. (1999). Stereotype threat and women's math performance. *Journal of Experimental Social Psychology* 35: 4–28.

Steele, C. M., and Aronson, J. (1995). Stereotype threat and the intellectual test performance of African Americans. *Journal of Personality and Social Psychology* 69: 797–811.

Steele, C. M., Spencer, S. J., and Aronson, J. (2002). Contending with group image: The psychology of stereotype threat and social identity threat. *Advances in Experimental Social Psychology* 34: 379–440.

Stichting Gay and Lesbian Games (1998). Gay Games Amsterdam 1998: Official program. Archived at Victoria University. Caroline Symons personal archive.

Sydney Games (2002a). Gay Games VI: Official guide. Archived at Victoria University. Caroline Symons personal archive.

——— (2002b). Sydney 2002: Gay Games VI gender policy (final), adopted 10 July. Archived at Victoria University. Caroline Symons personal archive.

Symons, C. (2002). The Gay Games and community. In D. Hemphill and C. Symons (eds.), *Gender, sexuality, and sport: A dangerous mix* (pp. 100–117). Petersham, NSW: Walla Walla.

——— (2004). *The Gay Games: The play of sexuality, sport and community.* PhD diss. Melbourne: Victoria University.

——— (2010). *The Gay Games: A history.* London: Routledge.

Symons, C., and Hemphill, D. (2006). Transgendering sex and sport in the Gay Games. In J. Caudwell (ed.), *Sport, sexualities, and queer/theory* (pp. 109–128). London: Routledge.

Symons, C., Sbraglia, M., Hillier, L., and Mitchell, M. (2010). *Come out to play. The sport experiences of lesbian, gay, bisexual, and transgender people in Victoria.* Melbourne: ISEAL.

Tajfel, H., and Turner, J. C. (1979). An integrative theory of intergroup conflict. In W. G. Austin and S. Worchel (eds.), *The social psychology of intergroup relations* (pp. 33–47). Monterey, CA: Brooks/Cole.

Team Berlin. (2009). Open letter to the board of the Federation of Gay Games. September 30. Archived at Victoria University. Caroline Symons personal archive.

Thurlow, C. (2001). Naming the "outsider within": Homophobic pejoratives and the verbal abuse of LGB high-school pupils. *Journal of Adolescence* 24: 25–38.

Tilly, C. (1978). *From mobilization to revolution.* Reading, MA: Addison-Wesley.

Timanus, E. (2010). Stanford locks up Directors' Cup award for 16th consecutive season. *USA Today,* June 22. http://www .usatoday.com/sports/college/2010-06-22-stanford-directors -cup_N.htm.

Torre, P. S., and Epstein, D. (2012). The transgender athlete. *Sports Illustrated,* May 28. http://sportsillustrated.cnn.com/vault/article /magazine/MAG1198744/index.htm.

Tsui, A. S., Egan, T. D., and O'Reilly, C. A., III (1992). Being different: Relational demography and organizational attachment. *Administrative Science Quarterly* 37: 549–579.

Turner, J. C., Hogg, M. A., Oakes, P. J., Reicher, S. D., and Wetherell, M. S. (1987). *Rediscovering the social group: A self-categorization theory.* Oxford: Blackwell.

Unity '94 (1994a). Operations report. Archived at San Francisco Public Library. Federation of Gay Games Archive, Box 5, Series IV, Gay Games IV, Folder 46.

——— (1994b). Special needs are human needs. Archived at San Francisco Public Library. Federation of Gay Games Archive, Box 2, Series IV, Gay Games IV, Folder 56.

van Knippenberg, D., De Dreu, C. K. W., and Homan, A. C. (2004). Work group diversity and group performance: An integrative model and research agenda. *Journal of Applied Psychology* 89: 1008–1022.

van Knippenberg, D., and Haslam, S. A. (2003). Realizing the diversity dividend: Exploring the subtle interplay between identity, ideology, and reality. In S. A. Haslam, D. van Knippenberg, M. J. Platow, and N. Ellemers (eds.), *Social identity at work: Developing theory for organizational practice* (pp. 61–77). New York: Psychology Press.

van Knippenberg, D., Haslam, S. A., and Platow, M. J. (2007). Unity through diversity: Value-in-diversity beliefs, work group diversity, and group identification. *Group Dynamics: Theory, Research, and Practice* 11: 207–222.

van Knippenberg, D., and Schippers, M. C. (2007). Work group diversity. *Annual Review of Psychology* 58: 515–541.

van Leeuwen, I. (1998). *Gay Games Amsterdam 1998: Equal gay and lesbian event? Efforts of the feminine politics.* Amsterdam: Gay Games Amsterdam.

Vaux, A. (1988). *Social support: Theory, research, and intervention.* New York: Praeger.

Wackwitz, L. A. (2003). Verifying the myth: Olympic sex testing and the category "woman." *Women's Studies International Forum* 26: 553–560.

Waddell, T. (1986). Thinking out loud. *Coming Up* 7 (11) (August): 8.

Wahl, G. (2011). Christie Rampone adds a special story to U.S. Women's Cup quest—Grant Wahl. http://sportsillustrated.cnn.com/2011/writers/grant_wahl/07/16/wwc.final.preview/index.html.

Waitt, G. (2006). Boundaries of desire: Becoming sexual through the spaces of Sydney's 2002 Gay Games. *Annual Association of American Geographers* 96 (4): 773–787.

Walker, N. A., and Bopp, T. (2011). The underrepresentation of women in the male dominated sport workplace: Perspectives of female coaches. *Journal of Workplace Rights* 15 (1): 47–64.

Walker, N. A., Bopp, T., and Sagas, M. (2011). Gender bias in the perception of women as collegiate men's basketball coaches. *Journal for the Study of Sports and Athletes in Education* 5 (2): 157–176.

Warwick, I., Aggleton, P., and Douglas, N. (2001). Playing it safe: Addressing the emotional and physical health of lesbian and gay pupils in the U.K. *Journal of Adolescence* 24: 129–140.

Washington, M., and Patterson, K. D. W. (2011). Hostile takeover or joint venture: Connections between institutional theory and sport management research. *Sport Management Review* 14: 1–12.

Weeks, J. (2007). *The world we have won.* London: Routledge.

Weinberg, G. (1972). *Society and the healthy homosexual.* New York: St. Martin's.

Weinberg, T. S. (1994). *Gay men, drinking, and alcoholism.* Carbondale: Southern Illinois University Press.

Whisenant, W. A., Pedersen, P. M., and Obenour, B. L. (2002). Success and gender: Determining the rate of advancement for intercollegiate athletic directors. *Sex Roles* 47 (9–10): 485–491.

WIAA (Washington Interscholastic Athletic Association) (2010). 2010–2011 official handbook. http://www.wiaa.com/ConDocs/Con358/Eligibility.pdf.

Williams, K., Haywood, K., and Painter, M. (1996). Environmental versus biological influences on gender differences in overarm throw for force: Dominant and non-dominant arms. *Women Sport & Physical Activity Journal* 5: 29–50.

Williams, R. (1977). *Marxism and literature.* Oxford: Oxford University Press.

Williams, R. (1985). *Keywords: A vocabulary of culture and society.* Oxford: Oxford University Press.

Wolf Wendel, L., Toma, J. D., and Morphew, C. (2001). How much difference is too much difference? Perceptions of gay men and lesbians in intercollegiate athletics. *Journal of College Student Development* 42 (5): 465–479.

Woog, D. (2011). Keelin Godsey has a hammer. *South Florida Gay News,* January 3. http://www.southfloridagaynews.com/life -and-style/sports/2826-the-outfield-keelin-godsey-has-a -hammer.html.

Worthen, M. G. F. (forthcoming). An argument for separate analyses of attitudes toward lesbian, gay, bisexual men, bisexual women, MtF and FtM transgender individuals. *Sex Roles.*

W-PATH (World Professional Association for Transgender Health) (2001). The Harry Benjamin International Gender Dysphoria Association's standards of care for gender identity disorders. 6th version. http://www.wpath.org/publications_standards.cfm.

Zgonc, E. (2010). 1999/2000–2008/2009 NCAA student-athlete ethnicity report. Indianapolis: National Collegiate Athletic Association.

Zipp, J. F. (2011). Sport and sexuality: Athletic participation by sexual minority and sexual majority adolescents in the U.S. *Sex Roles* 64: 19–31.

The Contributors

Eric Anderson is an American sociologist at the University of Winchester in England. His research focuses on sexualities and masculinities, particularly concerning sport and relationships. He is author of books such as *In the Game: Gay Athletes and the Cult of Masculinity*, and *Sport, Masculinities, and Sexualities*.

Erin E. Buzuvis is professor of law at Western New England University School of Law. Buzuvis researches and writes about gender and discrimination in sport, including intersecting sexual orientation and race discrimination in women's athletics, retaliation against coaches in collegiate women's sports, and the role of interest surveys in Title IX compliance. Buzuvis currently serves as director of the Center for Gender and Sexuality Studies at Western New England University School of Law. She also teaches courses on administrative law, employment discrimination, Title IX, torts, and property, and she is a cofounder and contributor to the Title IX Blog.

George B. Cunningham is professor of sport management and the associate dean for academic affairs in the College of Education and Human Development at Texas A&M University. His research focuses on diversity, group processes, and employee attitudes. He is the author of numerous journal articles and the book *Diversity in Sport Organizations*.

Mark McCormack is a lecturer at Durham University, England. His research examines the changing nature of masculinities and sexual identities in cultures of decreased homophobia. He has published in a range of international journals and is author of *The Declining Significance of Homophobia*.

E. Nicole Melton is assistant professor of sport administration and leadership at Seattle University. Her scholarship focuses on diversity and inclusion in sport and sport organizations. Melton has published in prominent academic journals, authored book chapters, and presented at national conferences.

Matthew Ripley is a sociologist based at the University of Winchester, England. His research focuses on the intersection of sport, masculinity, and sexuality. He has been published in multiple internationally recognized journals.

Melanie L. Sartore-Baldwin is assistant professor of kinesiology at East Carolina University. Her research addresses issues of diversity and social justice as they relate to sport and organizations. Her primary areas of research include weight, race, sex and gender, and sexual orientation within sport.

Caroline Symons is senior lecturer in sport event management, and ethics and social policy in sport at Victoria University. Her research focuses on gender and diversity in sport, community sport management, and participation and social policy in sport. She is author of *The Gay Games: A History*.

Nefertiti A. Walker is assistant professor of sport management at the University of Massachusetts, Amherst. Her research interest lies in examining underrepresented groups in sport, such as women, sexual minorities, and ethnic/racial minorities. She is an advocate for inclusivity and currently serves as the vice president of inclusion and social justice for the National Association for Girls and Women in Sport.

Index

About the Book

What does it mean to be gay, lesbian—or anyone else considered a sexual "other"—in the arena of competitive sport? With what consequences? The authors of *Sexual Minorities in Sports* shed light on the dynamics of sexual prejudice in venues ranging from high school athletics to the Olympics and the major leagues. Case studies of the experiences of LGBT athletes, coaches, and administrators also take account of the important role of race.

Empirically rich and full of theoretical insights, the book concludes by pinpointing opportunities for confronting prejudice and empowering individuals across the lines of both gender and sexual orientation.

Melanie L. Sartore-Baldwin is assistant professor of kinesiology at East Carolina University.